Fashion Design & Illustration

Fashion Design & Illustration 1

Basic guidelines

John M. Turnpenny

Hutchinson
London Melbourne Sydney Auckland Johannesburg

Hutchinson Education

An imprint of Century Hutchinson Limited

62–65 Chandos Place, London WC2N 4NW

Century Hutchinson Australia Pty Ltd
PO Box 496, 16–22 Church Street, Hawthorn, Victoria 3122, Australia

Century Hutchinson New Zealand Limited
PO Box 40–086, Glenfield, Auckland 10, New Zealand

Century Hutchinson South Africa (Pty) Ltd
PO Box 337, Bergvlei 2012, South Africa

First published 1981
Reprinted 1982, 1983, 1986, 1987

Set in Helios

Typeset and originated by Ebenezer Baylis & Son Ltd
The Trinity Press, Worcester, and London
Printed and bound in Great Britain by
Anchor Brendon Ltd, Tiptree, Essex

British Library Cataloguing in Publication Data
Turnpenny, John
    Fashion design and illustration
    1. Costume design
    I. Title
    746.9′2   TT507

ISBN 0 09 143521 8

Contents

Introduction

I am presenting this book as a guide to would-be fashion designers and fashion artists, together with a definition of the approach that is required for each area. As far as space allows I have attempted to illustrate the processes we recommend step by step, as this is what is frequently asked of me by students. I have spent many years in industry and some twelve years teaching this subject. In that time I have had plenty of opportunity to observe the 'rag trade' from a number of different angles.

Many aspiring fashion designers have completely the wrong idea of how the fashion trade works. I hope this book may be of some help and guidance in correcting misconceptions. New art and design courses are being developed and old ones are changing structure. For the majority of students a sound basic college training is still the best approach before plunging into fashion drawing or fashion design. Of course it all depends how students use a college fashion course. They should acquire all the basic knowledge of this subject. They must then be prepared to adapt themselves to their individual firms' requirements.

Designers must also now consider the effects of rapid changes accelerating within the clothing trade, with the increase in automation and development of computer-aided design, together with the growing importance of fashion marketing and merchandizing.

Design training

As in many professions today, the role of fashion designer is highly competitive and an aspiring designer is advised to attend a recognized college course of diploma or degree status, and before this to do at least a one year foundation course.

There are, of course, exceptions to this statement but today's designer must develop a 'professional' approach and the school of art and design is the best grounding for such skills. Fashion design is gradually acquiring more prestige and fashion degrees are now awarded in several colleges, as in other areas of industrial design. However, there are still many in the rag trade who would dismiss the idea of a degree in fashion as being quite irrelevant.

We who teach this subject are often accused by the trade of spending too much time drawing pretty faces, but I have noticed that on several occasions when asked to judge a competition, the trade invariably selects the prettiest or most striking sketch and not necessarily the best design. Students may often have to compete in competitions and bursaries and naturally a high standard of presentation is required. For example, one would hardly expect a designer of cars to present his ideas in any but the most sophisticated form.

Therefore, students must acquire the necessary techniques and skills in order to present their ideas to the best advantage. On graduation they must show they are able to design for various markets and can work within various constraints, as well as illustrating their creative ability and showing how they arrived at their final conclusions.

On our design courses we do appreciate that once employed in industry, fashion designers have little time for finished design work; in fact, in operation, the buyer often only requires a quick sketch, which may amount to no more than a variation of a garment already in the range.

The simplest way of putting over an idea is to do a sketch, rather than laboriously describing the idea or making a sample. If a designer must communicate to a buyer in a hurry, obviously an ability to draw the idea in an attractive manner is a great asset. Also, as a freelance designer, one could not carry masses of garments about and so a portfolio of designs is necessary.

When designers leave their art school or college they should indicate clearly by the professional appearance of their work, and all the back up work that goes with it, that they have reached a certain standard, just as any other industrial designer would do.

There are few really great fashion innovators – truly creative talents who give a new lead and direction. However, there is much creative work produced following the lead given by a brilliant designer, such as Kenzo or Cardin, and there is a vast area of design 'adaptation' within certain constraints for various levels of trade.

A designer must develop a sound colour sense. Reputations have been enhanced by this aspect of design as, for example, in the Biba look (Barbara Hulanicki). Incidentally, she started as a very good fashion artist.

Also a keen appreciation of the character of a fabric is imperative. This is where many students go wrong. They do not design for the fabric but make the fabric do something alien to its nature. Colour, texture, balance and proportion, decoration and details, all these things, as well as skills of cutting and draping, must be studied in depth. At the same time the student should be pursuing studies that lead to new sources of inspiration and creative thinking.

Students must also learn how to make the garment as they must be able to inform the sample hand how the various pieces sew together, suggesting alterations where necessary if a design as produced in a prototype is going to be difficult in manufacture. Many machinists are paid on a piece rate and must be able to produce the garment in a reasonable time without too many problems. In industry the designer must work very closely with the sample machinist and, in the majority of cases, be able to produce a sound commercial flat pattern and costing, and in some cases be able to grade the various sizes. Grading, however, is mostly done by a specialist as this is very important if the 'image' of the style is to be retained throughout the size range. Therefore a very important element of the learning process is to be able to 'translate' a style line from a sketch to a 'flat' pattern, as well as developing an ability to drape. A knowledge of grading is advisable. The aim is that everything produced as a sketch should be able to be produced in three-dimensional form. Many beginners produce ideas on paper that will not work when they are made up in garment form.

Most designers work from a block and the student learns how to construct a block, although one is usually provided in industry. Each firm tends to have its own ideas on blocks. A block is virtually a second 'shell' or case of the torso of a given size, in flat pattern form. There are sleeve and skirt blocks as well. One rarely has to construct a new block in industry; it is usually a question of adaptation. On occasions I have had to construct new knitwear blocks and children's blocks, but this is unusual. The amount of tolerance varies from firm to firm. This can be a sore point with some shops as they complain that two garments of the same size fitting and similar style can be so different in actual fitting.

Design training (continued)

Many design schools work on specific project work in the second year – say for six weeks – where a student will be set a design project with certain fabrics or be given a design brief for a specific market or area. Quite often this is tied up with an actual manufacturer who will then come into the school and take part in an assessment and criticism of the finished garment.

This is excellent practice for a student as it often entails working within set constraints and limited yardage. It also affords the opportunity to use a wide cross-section of fabrics and learn how they react in make-up. Also there is the opportunity to experiment, for example, with children's wear, casual wear, knitwear, menswear, outsizes, etc.

Also art schools and colleges are grateful for the support of industry in working on competitions where, in addition to financial reward, the fabric is often provided by the firms concerned. Naturally schools have a limited amount of money to spend on providing fabric and so one has often to use synthetics or mixture fabrics, as pure woollens, silks, etc., become too expensive. Here the study of textiles is very important and collections of fabrics should be made. Design projects can be based on such collections, together with market research of the particular level of trade or area aimed at. Again this helps the student to recognize the essential character of a fabric and judge whether it is suitable for that market or level of trade.

Embroidery, surface decoration, millinery and knitwear are all usually part of a fashion design course, as well as the business aspects of the fashion trade.

The latter is very important, as many students have vague hopes of starting their own businesses and 'doing their own thing'. They do not realize how many facets there are to running a business; that somewhere along the line someone must like their work enough to buy it and come back for more; and that it must be produced at a price that is competitive. Far too many designers and boutiques have started with a bang and then fizzled out because they could not maintain the first impact and became bogged down by production problems and cost factors. Innovative individuality is great, but it occupies only a small part of the fashion trade. Most designers have to work on the current fashion wavelength and produce individual 'looks' around a theme. The more talented designers feel instinctively what trends lie ahead and so their work looks 'new' and fresh in its approach. Students should be wary of going against the movement of fashion for they may find that their work just does not sell.

Usually, by the time students have reached their final year of a fashion course they have a good idea

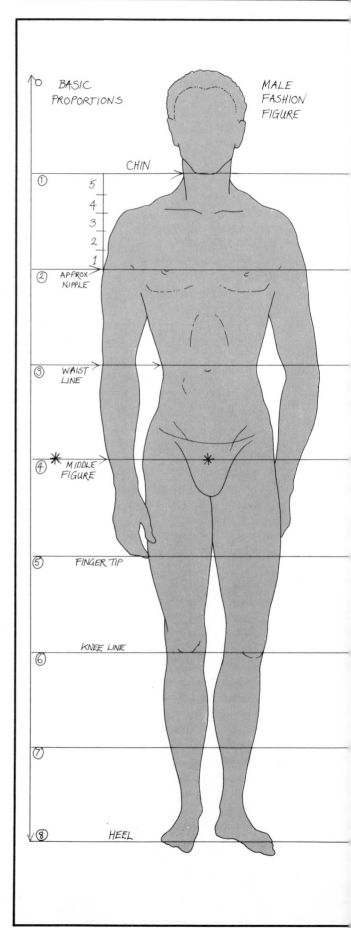

BASIC PROPORTIONS

MALE FASHION FIGURE

CHIN

① 5 4 3 2 1

② APPROX NIPPLE

③ WAIST LINE

④ MIDDLE FIGURE

⑤ FINGER TIP

KNEE LINE

⑥

⑦

⑧ HEEL

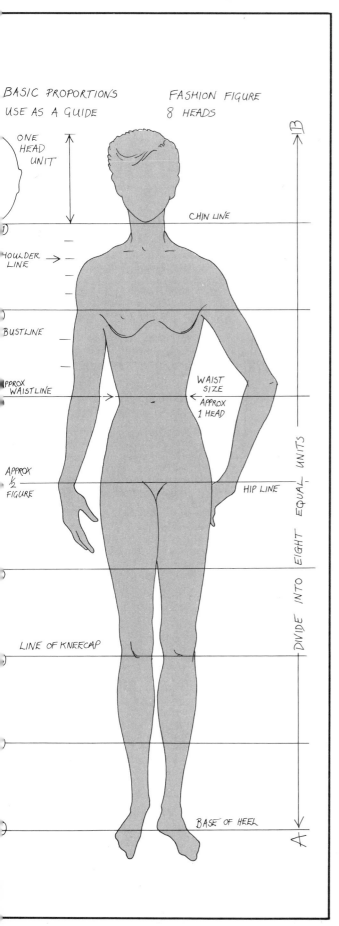

BASIC PROPORTIONS
USE AS A GUIDE

FASHION FIGURE
8 HEADS

ONE
HEAD
UNIT

CHIN LINE

SHOULDER
LINE

BUSTLINE

APPROX
WAISTLINE

WAIST
SIZE
APPROX
1 HEAD

APPROX
½
FIGURE

HIP LINE

DIVIDE INTO EIGHT EQUAL UNITS

LINE OF KNEECAP

BASE OF HEEL

of the area in which they want to specialize and so they concentrate on this. However, they should produce evidence that they can design for other areas as well. A collection of garments should be produced comprising three or four ensembles projecting the student's conception of a look or a theme. The accent should be on a creative approach while showing that they are aware that modifications might be necessary should the garments go into production. At this stage, as the accent is on the creative approach, I often get this kind of comment from a manufacturer: 'OK, fine, but why can't they produce something interesting from three metres!' This is rather a difficult problem, as one cannot restrict a student all along the line and then expect him to develop a creative approach. I think some manufacturers, who are obviously concerned with the cost factor, tend to overlook this element of design training.

The problem that teachers of fashion design often encounter is that the student prefers to do drawings rather than pursue the concept through to the finished garment. This can be overcome to a large extent by designing in a sample room situation. The position of design tutors is not easy. They must at no point stifle the creative instinct and yet, at the same time, they must develop an awareness in the student of the complexities of the rag trade. Students must also learn to assimilate various and differing opinions and criticisms of their work and only then decide what is right for them. If they can do that, they can break all the rules with conviction and authority, confidence and style.

Obviously some students have more innate ability to draw than others, but there are ways in which diagrammatic sketches can be presented attractively and convincingly if draughtsmanship is weak. These things must be accepted, analysed and worked on. They must recognize their limitations.

It is a part of most fashion courses to visit museums, fashion shows, galleries, etc., as this is an important part of the learning process. These visits should encourage the aspiring designer to look, think, and analyse, then create. One cannot create in a vacuum. In addition to being a very important stimulus for new design ideas, a spectacular exhibition of paintings can have a pronounced effect on the design of fabric and fashions.

This aspect of fashion design training is very important. A designer needs stimulus and needs to research into many and varied sources of inspiration in order to maintain a fresh and inventive approach. All too soon when involved in the day to day routine of a design post in industry, the pressures are such that one will only have time

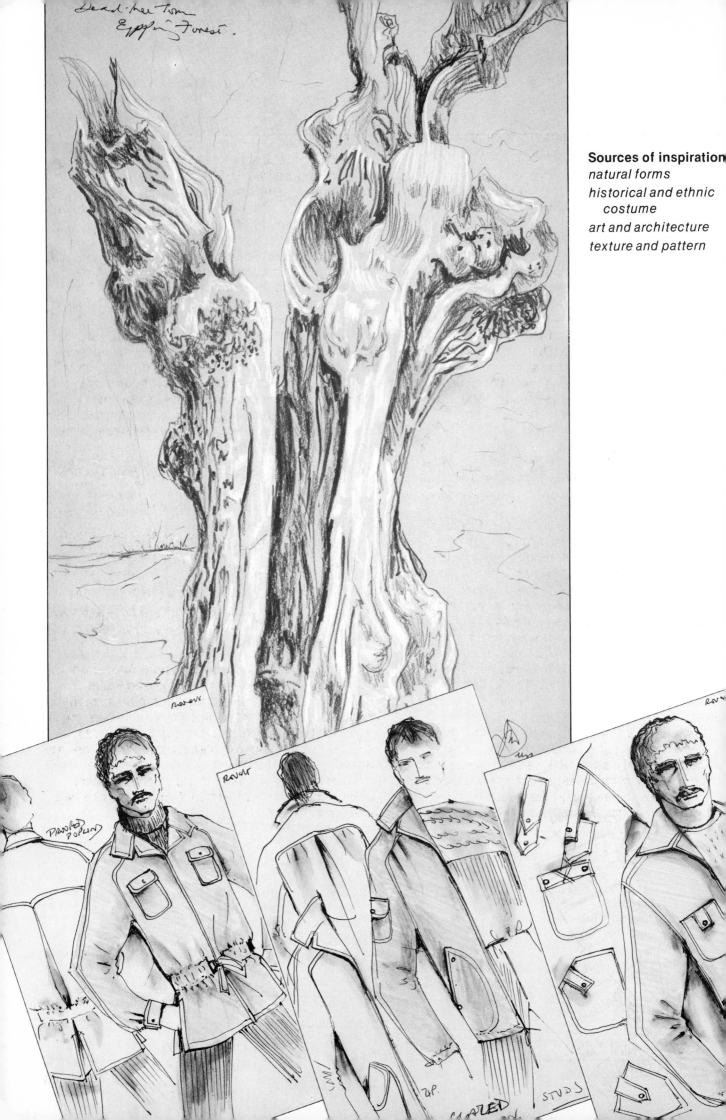

Sources of inspiration
natural forms
historical and ethnic
   costume
art and architecture
texture and pattern

for a quick visit to a trade show. Serious fashion designers must be attuned to developments in changes of taste and style in the arts generally if they are to sense how fashion is moving and evolving. They must also keep a wary eye on technological developments, for instance of new machinery for producing garments, as this may well alter the way a particular suit or dress has to be designed to fit in with the new processes. As in any other profession, a fashion designer should make an intensive study of the history of fashion and also study the work of past masters of the craft: Chanel, Balenciaga, Dior, etc., and analyse the reasons for their success.

From this brief outline the would-be fashion design student can see that there is much to be done, and so *to work* . . . .

Menswear

For the future designer of menswear the choice in training is somewhat limited, though this is a developing area.

Students with a particular interest in menswear quite often pursue a general fashion design course of three years and in the second year channel their project work into the menswear field. In the third and final year they would probably produce a volume of work with a weighting on menswear, but also indicating they have a potential for design in other areas, say knitwear or accessories. This is probably the most sensible approach as the first opportunity of working as a menswear designer may not easily present itself. It is only a form of self-preservation to show ability to work in other areas.

In menswear quite a lot of the design is done on a freelance basis, as small companies cannot afford to employ a full-time designer unless he can cope with some other aspect of the business.

In my own experience, I have found that some students who have completed a three year course in tailoring and mastered their craft, but only developed a certain limited design potential, then did a further intensive year in design, concentrating on a creative approach, and had the most gratifying results. They have a tremendous advantage for they have mastered all the techniques.

Few fashion courses can supplement their technical tutors with sample machinists and so, inevitably, most of the designs must be produced by the student concerned.

In menswear it is important for the aspiring designer to understand and be aware of market structures and various types of production, as this will often affect the design approach. Another development in menswear is the increasing importance of the role of design co-ordinator. Here several factors are involved and experience must be gained in all these areas:

Awareness of current trends – silhouette, shape, colour, fabrics, etc.
Analysis of sales – level of trading
Market research
Valuation of competition and prices – cost factor
Awareness of capabilities of making up – own factory or outworkers
Quality control – standard required
Presentation (image and style)
Assessment of any development in new machines which may change manufacturing processes and affect design approach

In fact, some menswear designers move from the area of management to design and some colleges have specialist courses in management with a design content. Students of menswear must decide if this may be another approach to gain access to the menswear design area if they are not strong in graphic skills.

Therefore in menswear design there is much more scope if, in addition to design flair, one can offer other skills.

Levels of trade

Haute couture has changed drastically in the past few years. Up to the late 1950s, *haute couture* was pre-eminent as the main source of fashion trends and their word was law. Now, many people affirm that the *prêt-à-porter* is a more lively and influential source of ideas. There are now few surviving British couturiers, as with the marked sociological changes of the last two decades there is no longer a clientele of sufficient numbers to maintain their position. As with his counterparts in Europe, a British couturier like Hardy Amies now acts as consultant designer in several areas. Worth (1825–94) is usually accepted as the first real couturier. He was English and may be regarded as the Establishment designer whereas Poiret, who designed more for the *demi-monde*, could be considered the opposite. Poiret had a tremendous impact on fashion, in that he persuaded women to discard the complicated corsets that were then worn and created a more fluid and yet dramatic effect. Using fabrics and decoration with an exotic and often oriental feeling, Poiret created a dramatic and striking silhouette.

Any serious student of fashion should also study the way Poiret encouraged famous artists like Matisse to co-operate with him in producing ideas for textiles. However, there were tremendous changes after the first world war and after the 1920s Poiret's influence waned as he became out of touch with changing life styles. Although he made a fortune in his lifetime, he died in penury on the French Riviera. More women were going out to work and the days had vanished when a woman could spend two or three hours on her toilette and change three or four times a day from morning outfit to afternoon gown or tea gown, then dinner or ball gown. Many people say couture is dead and I have heard it proposed by some experts in the history of fashion that in the near future we may find that, with air-conditioned cocooned cities, we shall wear more disposable clothing – possibly decorated tabards with some form of body garment. There are a considerable number of books that deal with couture – like *Paris Fashion* by Ruth Lynham and *In Vogue* by G. Howell – and they reveal a fascinating insight of how couture operates. An aspiring designer should study as many couturiers as possible, as many were superb masters of their craft.

Much discussion takes place about whether couture will survive at all in this world with ever-increasing competition and sociological changes in which fewer and fewer people can afford couture prices. However, the other side of the coin is that couturiers still do create a flow of ideas that manufacturers can copy, and often produce, and project a new image with an original use of fabrics that stimulates other designers. While we have a wealth of British talent, it does not seem to produce a look with the same authority as, say, St Laurent, that can be translated into mass fashion. Many people think couture may change in structure but not fade out completely. It is interesting to note how attitudes change in fashion within a few years. For example, Yves Saint Laurent, one of the most consistent innovators of the last two decades, now says he will hand over the design of the Rive Gauche collections to a team of designers, so that he can concentrate on his 'reborn' couture; whereas 20 years ago he was proclaiming that R.T.W. had taken over and couture was irrelevant. This is particularly noteworthy as we are beginning to see a reaction against the current influence of 'street fashion', which in many cases is extremely unattractive.

Many students often dream of opening their own fashion house and tend to forget the economics behind this. The experience of working in a couture house, however, can be invaluable but is not well paid.

Also, one is often working as part of a design team. At Cardin, for example, sixteen designers work on his various projects. Often a certain theme is given by the head or name designer and then the team must produce ideas to build up a certain look or theme. So young designers may have to restrict their own individual 'handwriting' in order to conform to the look of that particular collection.

There is, on the other hand, the opportunity to work with superb and costly fabrics and to learn intricate cutting techniques. Here, may I just add that if one is working in Paris or Rome it is most important to speak something of the language. There is a vast wealth of fabrics for a couturier to select from and three months before a collection, one will probably begin to visualize the fabrics one might use and then begin to assess the various ranges offered by the fabric houses. For example, we have had a decade of softer fabrics and now with the swing to stiffer fabrics, like moiré, poult, brocade, satin, ottoman, etc., we have a more sculptured silhouette emerging. Very rarely a couturier may commission a fabric and there are only a few who design their own, such as Zandra Rhodes and Hanae Mori.

The production of a couture collection is now fantastically expensive and is used, at least in some cases, to keep the name in front of the public to aid the sale of ancillary products like perfume. Indeed it has been stated that the main reason Chanel re-opened after the war was to revitalize the sales of the Chanel perfumes. Consequently, few houses produce the huge collection seen in the 1950s when the couturier was still a powerful force in fashion.

The couturier will probably have decided on certain themes and will give these trend sketches to his team to develop and produce the toiles.

The toile is the original idea of a garment made in calico. Obviously if one is working in very expensive fabrics it would be foolish to make a mistake and often these toiles change several times before the correct silhouette, proportion of detail, balance, etc., has been achieved. I have often seen garments at Balenciaga where a movement of 0.5 cm in a seam would make all the difference and it is this perfection of cut and balance for which couture is renowned. There is also a total disregard for the amount of fabric used as long as the effect is totally successful and a beautiful garment is produced.

Medium and mass production
Designing for mass production can be very demanding, for the challenge is often to produce an interesting and exciting garment from a small yardage and minimum work content, as opposed to couture where the total effect is all important and cost secondary.

Now that many ideas spring from the *prêt-à-porter* and the inexpensive side of the market, we get a more lively look often aimed at the younger set.

In designing for mass production one must consider the market one is aiming at, the cost factor, the type of make-up available, work content, fabric analysis, hanger appeal, etc. Also, if producing for very large multiples, the buyer will probably have definite views on certain styles required each season and may have samples.

Certain firms will produce a range and if their name is well known and established, will not alter a particular design to suit a buyer, whereas smaller firms often have to do this. A buyer may change a detail of a selected style in the impression that she then obtains a more exclusive number. Buyers have a great deal of influence and can be quite powerful. It is often difficult for a student of fashion to appreciate this.

The designer usually works with the design director or sales director on the scope and type of the sampling programme. Once that is decided, they begin to look at fabric ranges from various manufacturers and to select small yardages for the first samples. Sometimes they may decide on certain basic fabric types which will probably appear in many designs so that the fabric can be ordered in bulk for forward delivery. Smaller companies can be much more flexible and they often produce new samples every week. If they sell them, they can buy fabric just to cover that order with no repeats.

As the range sampling proceeds, certain fabrics may be found to be more useful and others discarded, possibly because of make-up problems. If too many fabrics are used in various colour-ways, production problems often arise and so a style is usually offered in only two or three colour schemes. If you have several sizes and several colour schemes across a range, the permutations become immense and complicated. Some firms have frequent range meetings and change or modify a style or add a number quickly when they sense a new feeling developing as a trend. Other firms have their own individual 'handwriting' and a more restrained approach. The sales people know from the production side how many numbers or styles they can cope with in production. The designer works to this and is aware of the type of make-up in production.

In the majority of cases the designer and his assistant will produce the sample and first patterns, usually co-operating closely with the sample machinists and ironing out any tricky sewing problems which might cause havoc in the factory. Other staff usually cope with grading the various sizes and marker making, etc. Small companies often have two or three outworkers making up for them.

There are times when a designer may not like a particular fabric which the sales people believe is right and then he or she must overcome their dislike and produce something that the trade would call 'smart and snappy'.

Designing for companies who sell to the large multiples can also mean working to a special size chart and producing sealed samples, where the production is often checked to the sealed sample. Here hanger appeal is often the first priority. However, many of these companies can pay very good salaries because of regular production. Some companies will also produce one range for the multiples and another more interesting range for up-market sales. More firms in the middle market are now producing an individual look and it is often very good experience for a young designer to start in this area. More and more people are also buying by mail-order, and in this area, if the order is very large, exclusivity will often be demanded. Also, some mail-order companies are now using well known designers as consultants. In the area of mass production garments, it is obvious therefore that aspiring designers must be able to cut a sound commercial pattern, know something of grading and be able to adapt their skills to the limitations and constraints of production or the individual look of that particular company.

British designers

The intention of this book being more to concentrate on techniques rather than to give a coverage of present fashion, I have not the space to cover all the wealth of British design talent. I can only mention and show examples of a few who have a distinct individual 'handwriting'.

John Bates for Jean Varon
Style 'singelese'. One-shouldered evening dress, fabric draped from shoulder and held with butterfly clasp and side split in skirt
Fabric – 100% polyester satin
Price £76 retail
Hat by Freddy Fox for John Bates

Emanuel
Day wear, 1979

Fabric:		
trousers	100% silk	£84
shirt	100% silk	£72
waistcoat	velvet	£53
jacket	bouclé wool	
	(velvet trim)	£210

Zandra Rhodes 1976

Sketch developed from a photograph by permission of David Bailey and by courtesy of *Vogue* magazine.

This sketch shows the effective use of a Zandra Rhodes print to give an elegant and glamorous evening look.

Technique

I used a tinted paper in order to show the effect of the pattern and translucent fabric. The folds were built up by use of half-tone wash, the highlights by use of white acrylic paint and the final detail with a black biro.

Yuki

Sketch developed from a photograph by permission of David Bailey and by courtesy of *Vogue* magazine.

This sketch shows the beautiful fluid quality of jersey fabric in the hands of a master designer like Yuki.

Technique
I used a black china marker and white pastel on a tinted paper.

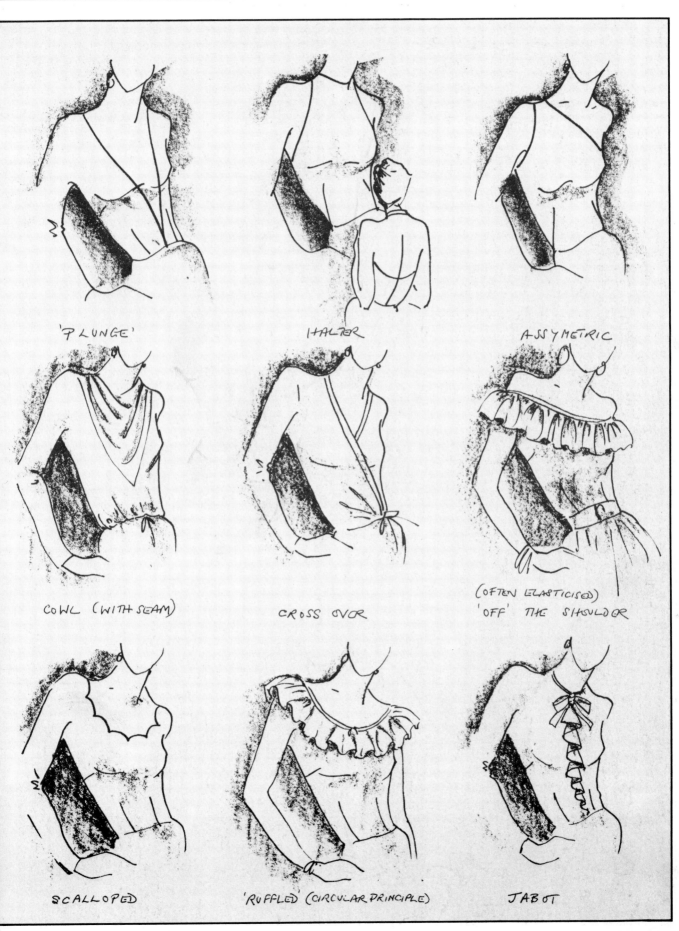

'PLUNGE'

HALTER

ASSYMETRIC

COWL (WITH SEAM)

CROSS OVER

(OFTEN ELASTICISED)
'OFF' THE SHOULDER

SCALLOPED

'RUFFLED' (CIRCULAR PRINCIPLE)

JABOT

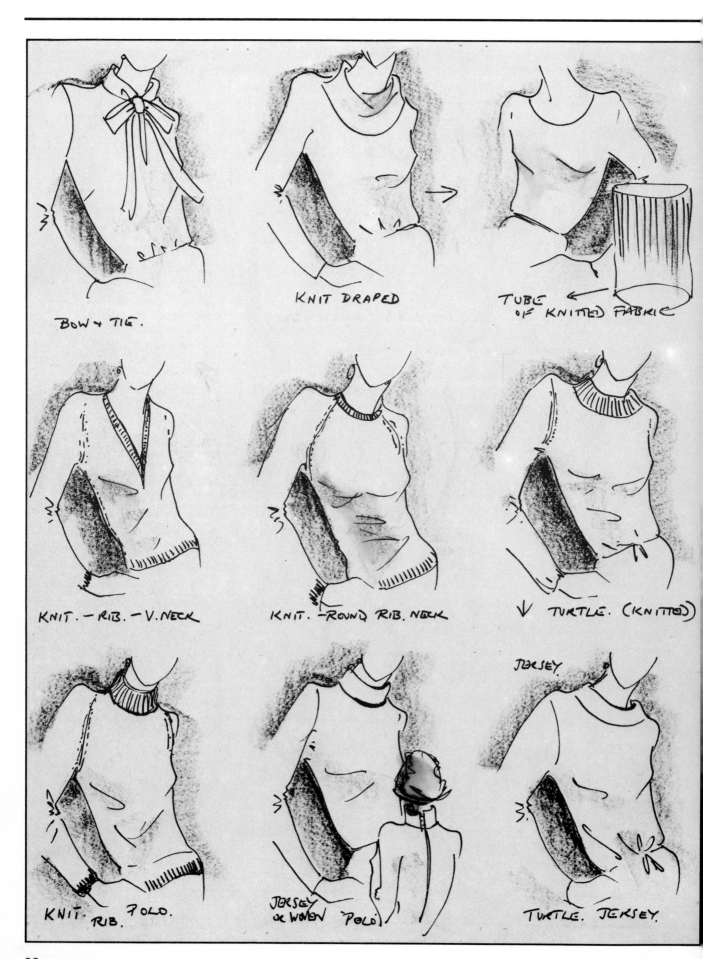

BOW & TIE.

KNIT DRAPED

TUBE OF KNITTED FABRIC

KNIT. — RIB. — V. NECK

KNIT. — ROUND RIB. NECK

↓ TURTLE. (KNITTED)

KNIT. RIB. POLO.

JERSEY OR WOVEN POLO

JERSEY

TURTLE. JERSEY.

Basic sleeves

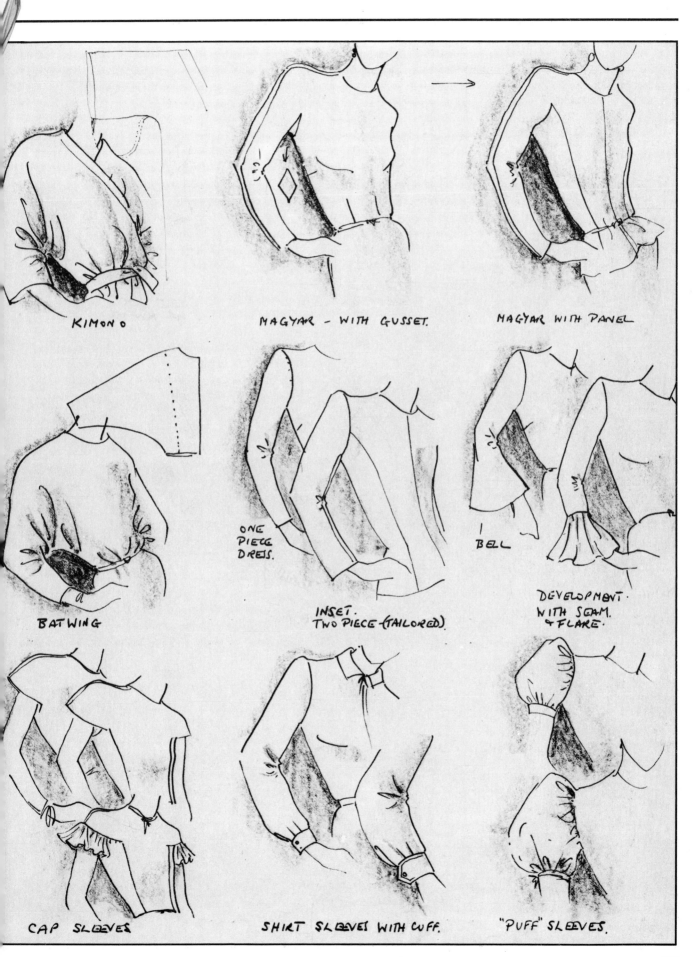

KIMONO

MAGYAR - WITH GUSSET.

MAGYAR WITH PANEL

BATWING

ONE PIECE DRESS.

INSET. TWO PIECE (TAILORED)

BELL

DEVELOPMENT. WITH SEAM. & FLARE.

CAP SLEEVES

SHIRT SLEEVES WITH CUFF.

"PUFF" SLEEVES.

Basic sleeves (continued)

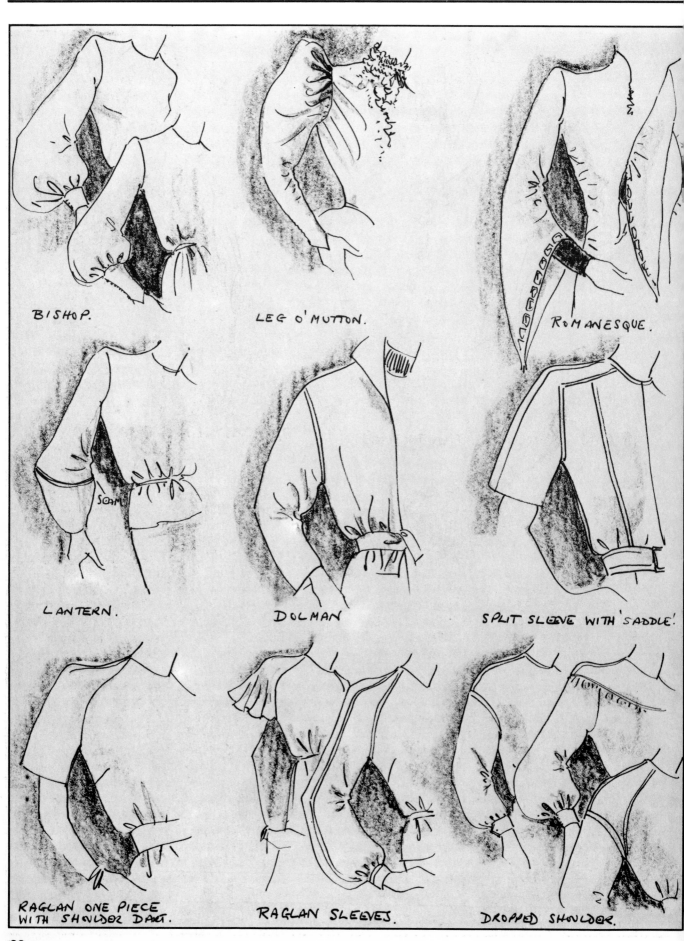

BISHOP.

LEG O'MUTTON.

ROMANESQUE.

LANTERN.

SEAM

DOLMAN

SPLIT SLEEVE WITH 'SADDLE'.

RAGLAN ONE PIECE WITH SHOULDER DART.

RAGLAN SLEEVES.

DROPPED SHOULDER.

Men's sleeve and shoulder variations

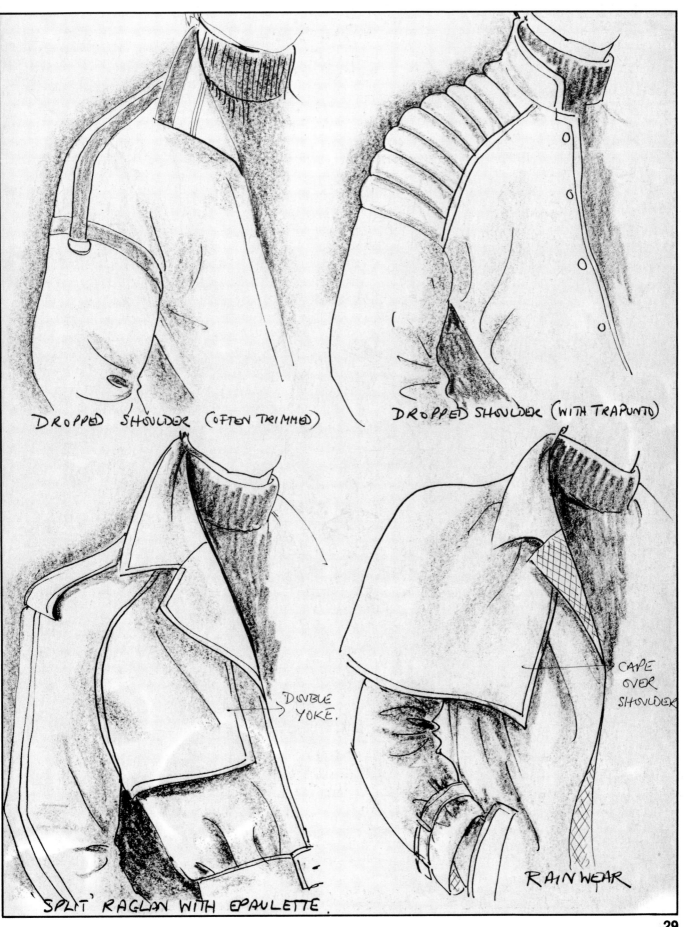

DROPPED SHOULDER (OFTEN TRIMMED)

DROPPED SHOULDER (WITH TRAPUNTO)

DOUBLE YOKE.

CAPE OVER SHOULDER

'SPLIT' RAGLAN WITH EPAULETTE.

RAINWEAR

Alternatives to button fastening

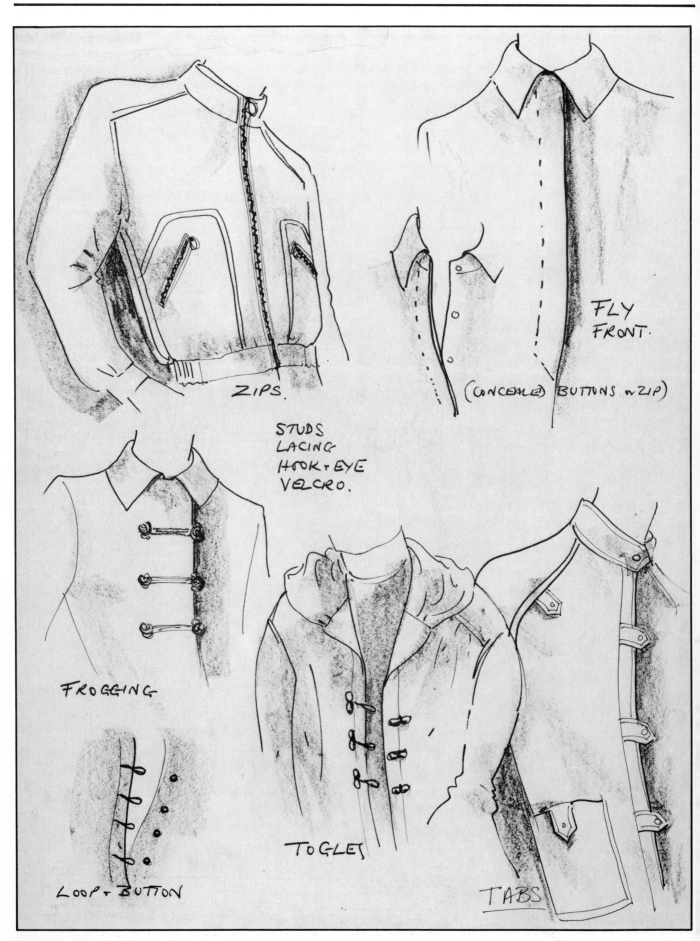

ZIPS.

FLY FRONT.

(CONCEALED BUTTONS or ZIP)

STUDS
LACING
HOOK + EYE
VELCRO.

FROGGING

LOOP + BUTTON

TOGGLE FASTENING

TABS

Basic skirts

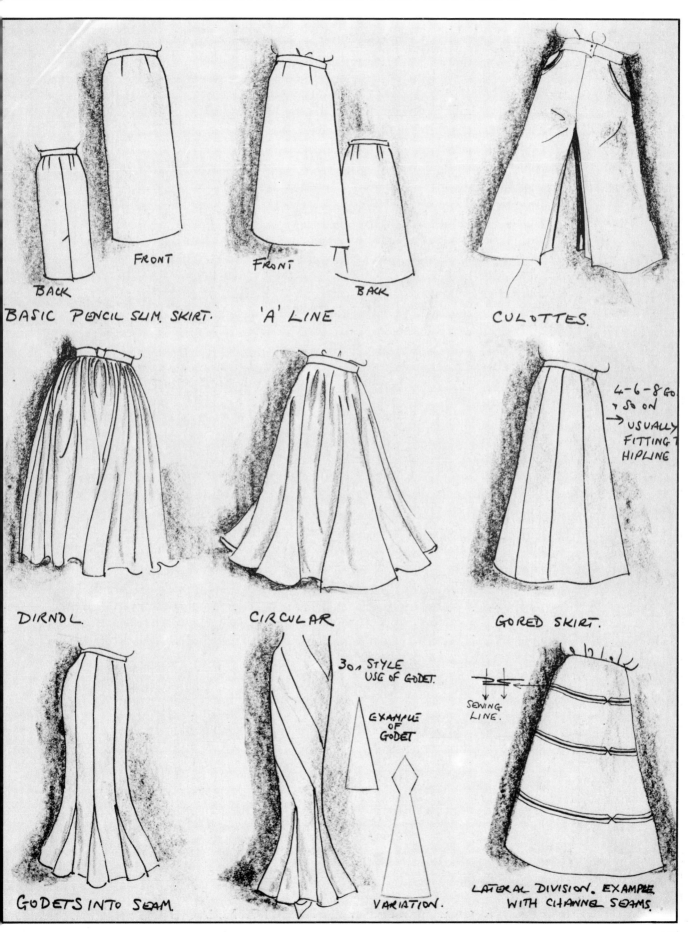

BASIC PENCIL SLIM. SKIRT.

BACK

FRONT

'A' LINE

FRONT

BACK

CULOTTES.

DIRNDL.

CIRCULAR

GORED SKIRT.

4-6-8 go & so on → USUALLY FITTING HIPLINE

GODETS INTO SEAM.

3 or STYLE USE OF GODET.

EXAMPLE OF GODET

VARIATION.

SEWING LINE.

LATERAL DIVISION. EXAMPLE WITH CHANNEL SEAMS.

Basic skirts (continued)

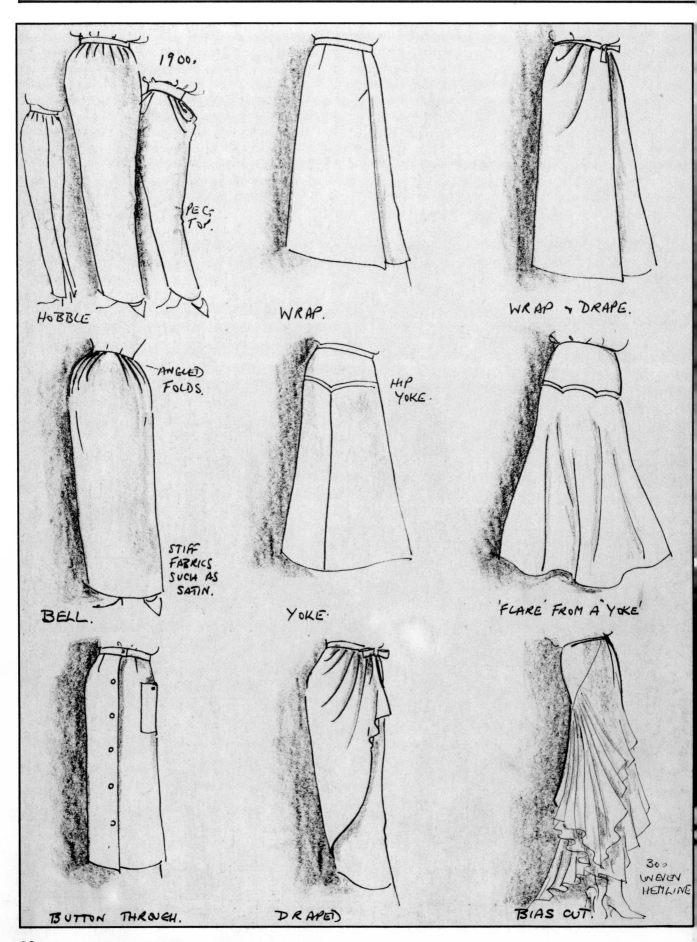

1900.

HOBBLE — PEG TOP.

WRAP.

WRAP & DRAPE.

BELL. — ANGLED FOLDS. — STIFF FABRICS SUCH AS SATIN.

YOKE. — HIP YOKE.

'FLARE' FROM A 'YOKE'

BUTTON THROUGH.

DRAPED.

BIAS CUT. — 30° UNEVEN HEMLINE

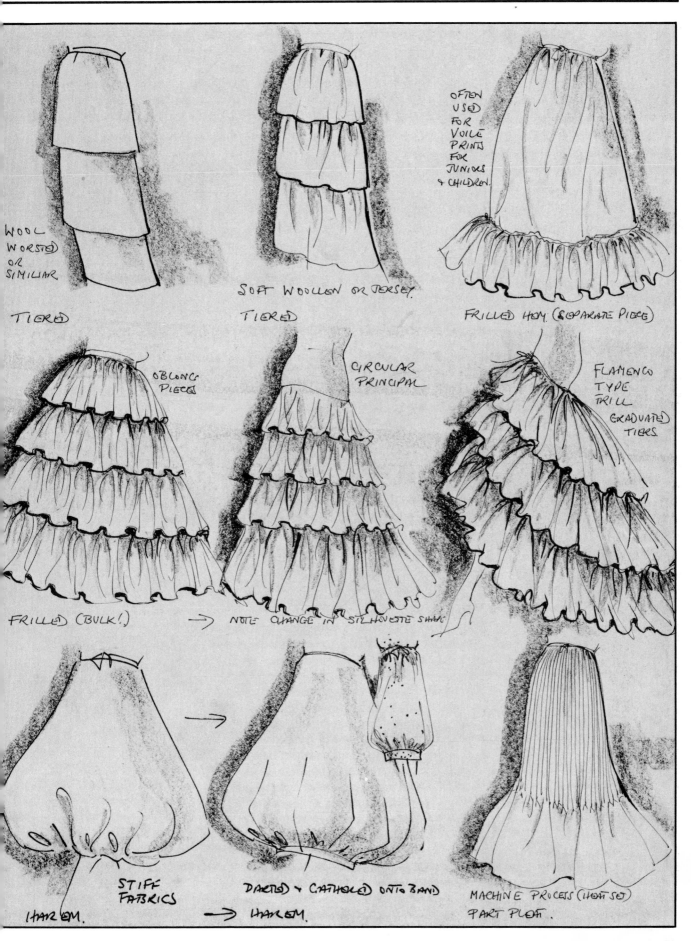

WOOL WORSTED OR SIMILIAR

TIERED

SOFT WOOLLEN OR JERSEY.

TIERED

OFTEN USED FOR VOILE PRINTS FOR JUNIORS & CHILDREN.

FRILLED HEM. (SEPARATE PIECE)

OBLONG PIECES

FRILLED (BULK!)

CIRCULAR PRINCIPAL

→ NOTE CHANGE IN SILHOUETTE SHAPE

FLAMENCO TYPE FRILL GRADUATED TIERS.

STIFF FABRICS

HAREM.

DARTED & GATHERED ONTO BAND

→ HAREM.

MACHINE PROCESS (HEAT SET) PART PLEAT.

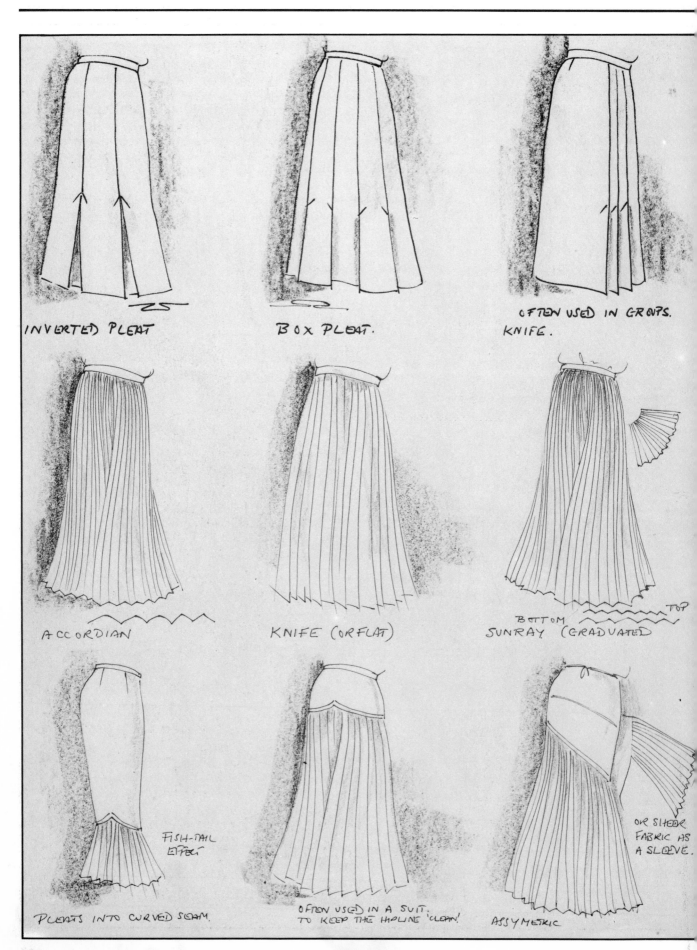

INVERTED PLEAT

BOX PLEAT.

OFTEN USED IN GROUPS.
KNIFE.

ACCORDIAN

KNIFE (OR FLAT)

BOTTOM
SUNRAY (GRADUATED
TOP

FISH-TAIL
EFFECT

PLEATS INTO CURVED SEAM.

OFTEN USED IN A SUIT.
TO KEEP THE HIPLINE 'CLEAN'

ASSYMETRIC

OR SHEER
FABRIC AS
A SLEEVE.

Experiment with variations on basic skirts

STITCHED DOWN
KNIFE PLEATS.

SMALL TUCKS RELEASED FROM M.
WAIST TO HIP CHANNEL SEAM.

'RELEASED' STITCHED HIP TUCKS. w PLEATS.

Basic collars

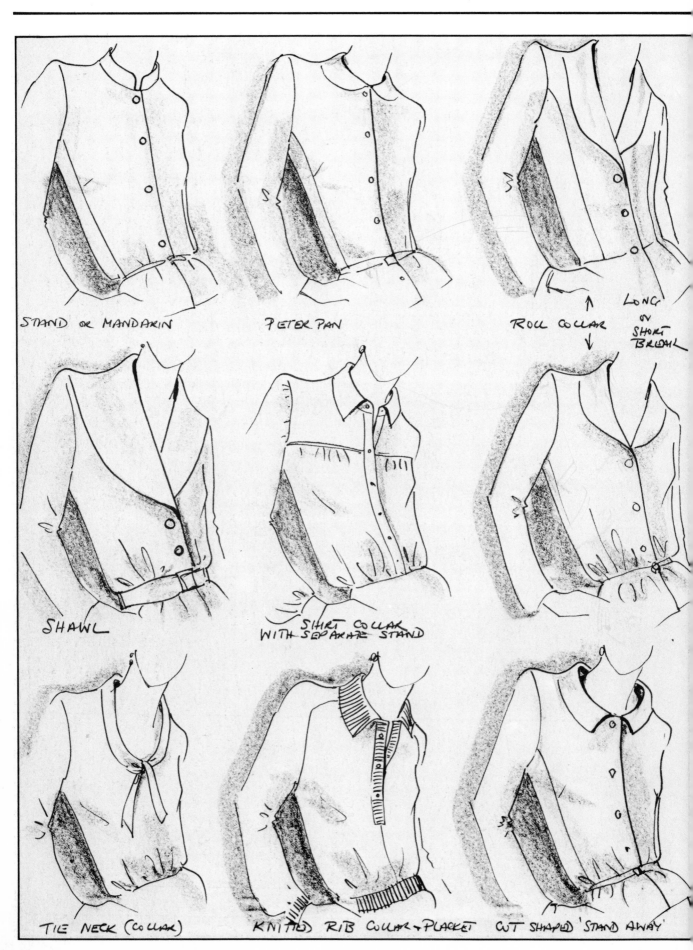

STAND OR MANDARIN

PETER PAN

ROLL COLLAR

LONG or SHORT BREAK

SHAWL

SHIRT COLLAR WITH SEPARATE STAND

TIE NECK (COLLAR)

KNITTED RIB COLLAR + PLACKET

CUT SHAPED 'STAND AWAY'

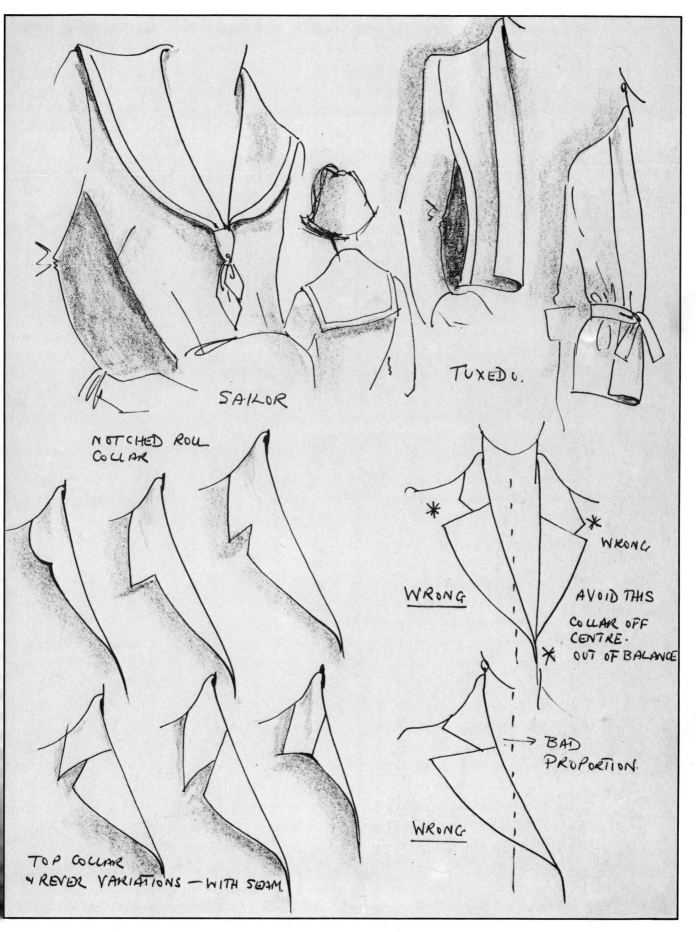

SAILOR

TUXEDO.

NOTCHED ROLL
COLLAR

TOP COLLAR
& REVER VARIATIONS — WITH SEAM.

WRONG

WRONG

AVOID THIS

COLLAR OFF
CENTRE.
OUT OF BALANCE

→ BAD
PROPORTION.

WRONG

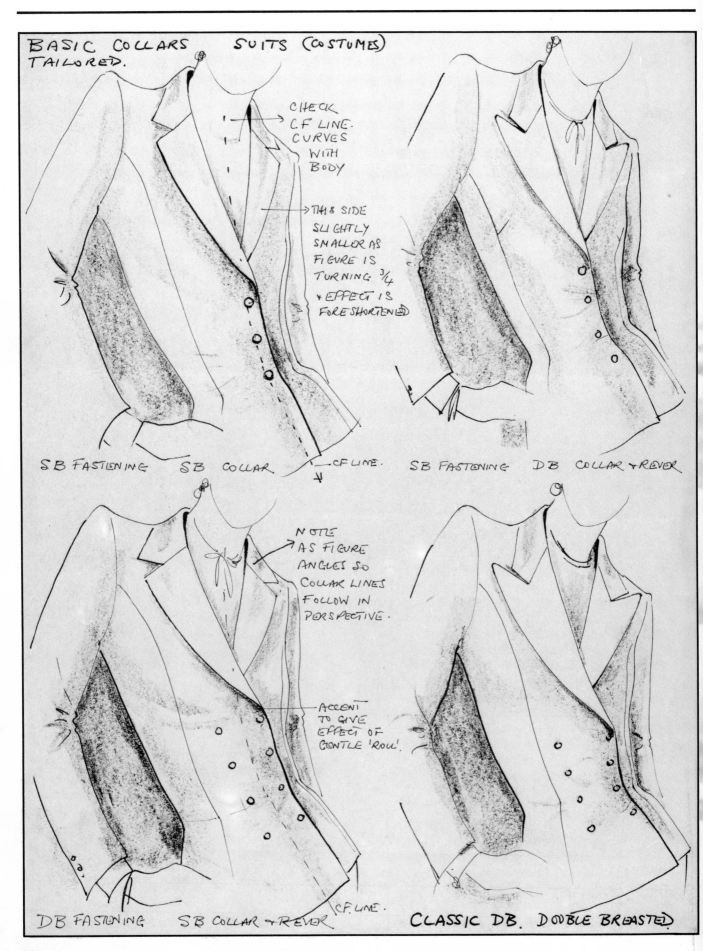

BASIC COLLARS SUITS (COSTUMES) TAILORED.

CHECK CF LINE. CURVES WITH BODY

→ THIS SIDE SLIGHTLY SMALLER AS FIGURE IS TURNING ¾ & EFFECT IS FORESHORTENED

SB FASTENING   SB COLLAR   — CF LINE.

SB FASTENING   DB COLLAR & REVER

NOTE AS FIGURE ANGLES SO COLLAR LINES FOLLOW IN PERSPECTIVE.

ACCENT TO GIVE EFFECT OF GENTLE 'ROLL'.

DB FASTENING   SB COLLAR & REVER   CF LINE.

CLASSIC DB. DOUBLE BREASTED

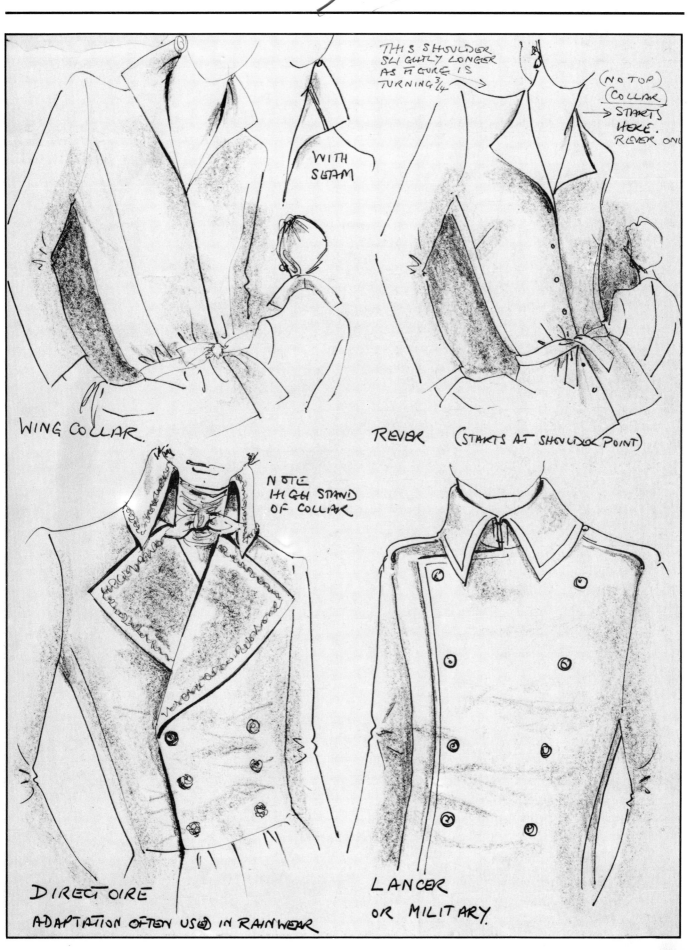

WITH SEAM

THIS SHOULDER SLIGHTLY LONGER AS FIGURE IS TURNING ¾

(NO TOP) (COLLAR) → STARTS HERE. REVER ONLY

WING COLLAR.

REVER (STARTS AT SHOULDER POINT)

NOTE HIGH STAND OF COLLAR

DIRECTOIRE

ADAPTATION OFTEN USED IN RAINWEAR

LANCER OR MILITARY.

Basic collar construction

BASIC COLLAR CONSTRUCTION.

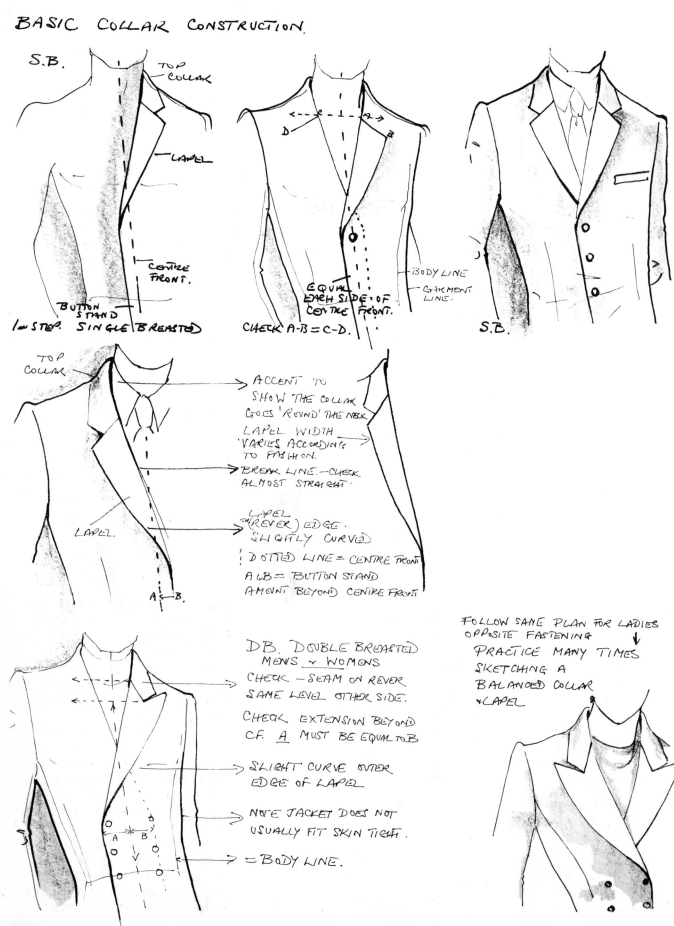

S.B.

TOP COLLAR

LAPEL

CENTRE FRONT.

BUTTON STAND

1ᵘ STEP. SINGLE BREASTED

EQUAL EACH SIDE OF CENTRE FRONT.

CHECK A-B = C-D.

BODY LINE
GARMENT LINE.

S.B.

TOP COLLAR

LAPEL.

A → B.

ACCENT TO SHOW THE COLLAR GOES 'ROUND' THE NECK

LAPEL WIDTH VARIES ACCORDING TO FASHION.

BREAK LINE. — CHECK ALMOST STRAIGHT.

LAPEL (REVER) EDGE. SLIGHTLY CURVED

DOTTED LINE = CENTRE FRONT
A ⊔ B = BUTTON STAND AMOUNT BEYOND CENTRE FRONT

DB. DOUBLE BREASTED MENS ∨ WOMENS

CHECK — SEAM ON REVER SAME LEVEL OTHER SIDE.

CHECK EXTENSION BEYOND C.F. A MUST BE EQUAL TO B

SLIGHT CURVE OUTER EDGE OF LAPEL

NOTE JACKET DOES NOT USUALLY FIT SKIN TIGHT.

= BODY LINE.

FOLLOW SAME PLAN FOR LADIES OPPOSITE FASTENING
PRACTICE MANY TIMES SKETCHING A BALANCED COLLAR + LAPEL

40

Decorative design

Decorative design is the opposite of structural design. It is applied surface decoration which does not fundamentally change the silhouette shape. However, many designers pursue a decorative approach and still create beautiful and satisfying fashions. Decoration can be employed in many ways, for example, embroidery, appliqué, pattern, stitch detail, lace, fur, braid, etc.

To illustrate a decorative approach I have shown a menswear casual wardrobe comprising beach separates, knitwear, blouson, tie, hat, duffel bag and semi-formal shirt, all using a zigzag chevron motif in a design development sheet.

Structural design

When studying aspects of structural design, it is most helpful for the student to compare silhouette shapes in historical costume. The cut of the garment determines the silhouette. The different placing of weight and volume achieved by pleats, tucks, gathers, folds, flare, etc., will radically change the silhouette shape. As fashion changes the silhouette changes. Analyse many fashion plates and try examples of blocking in to produce the silhouette shape. Compare different periods and note which fabrics are used. Examine how the shape changes.

A creative fashion innovator usually gives a lead with a new silhouette and therefore could well be called a structural designer, for example, Kenzo, Cardin, Dior and Balenciaga.

TUDOR

VICTORIAN. 1880

1979—
TREND TOWARDS
MORE BODY
FITTING
LINES.

STRETCH FABRIC
BODY FITTING
& LEOTARDS.

EMPIRE. 1804 -1815.

DIOR
NEW
19

Structural and decorative design

Raincoats
Note how the bold structural shape is enlivened by just the right proportion of detail and trim. Note also how the pose helps to emphasize the line of garment.

All detail is clearly shown and easy to read. For design sketches in the studio, I would add diagrammatic back views.

Courtesy of Nino publications.

Image
Smart casual showing a co-ordinated outfit of suit, shirt, shoes, etc.

Technique
Here I have used Caron d'Ache coloured pencils on a tinted paper. Experiment with water soluble Caron d'Ache, which can give a delicate wash or a strong tone. Then adapt your technique to the type of garment illustrated.

Decoration and detail

Fringe can be sporting or sophisticated as in dresses of the 1920s.

Thonging is usually associated with leather and suede and was originally used to hold garment pieces together.

Punching is also usually associated with suede and leather and can be used in an attractive decorative manner.

Ribbons and *feathers* must be used with discretion or they look overdone.

Trapunto has just been very fashionable with the emphasis on broad shoulders and is mainly applied with stiff fabrics and leather.

Smocking and *shirring* are quite often employed on young junior fashions and children's wear and can have interesting effects if the fabric is patterned.

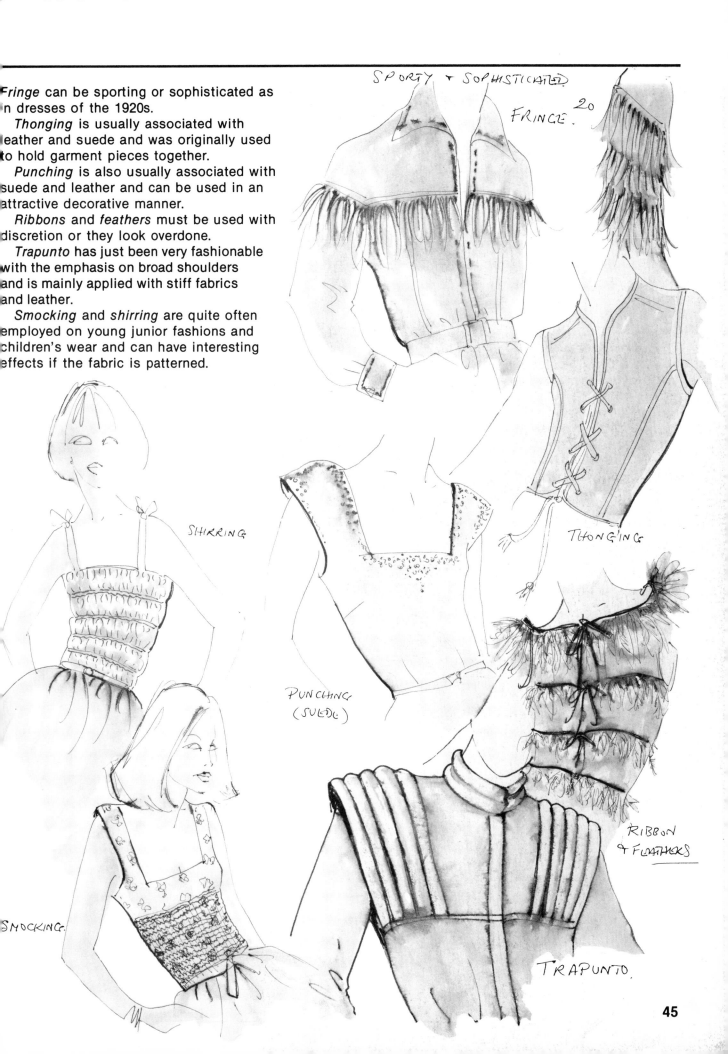

SPORTY + SOPHISTICATED FRINGE. 20

SHIRRING

THONG'ING

PUNCHING (SUEDE)

RIBBON & FEATHERS

SMOCKING.

TRAPUNTO.

45

Decoration and detail (continued)

Decorative seams are often used in tailored garments to emphasize a line or to bring interest to a severe shape.

Decorative stitching is employed in many ways, from the sporty to the dressy. Observe the effects on various fabrics, such as silk and wool.

Braid is often used to enliven a mass-produced garment.

Appliqué can be creative, but expensive in application, and so tends to be used on more expensive garments.

Groups of *pin tucks* can be very effective and are often used on OS sizes.

Flat tucks give an interesting change of texture.

Quilting comes and goes in fashion and is also being used in menswear now.

Piping is useful as an edge finish and as a feature using a contrasting colour.

Embroidery is also expensive and therefore appears on more expensive garments.

Try many experiments with all these, until you discover a fresh and exciting unusual application.

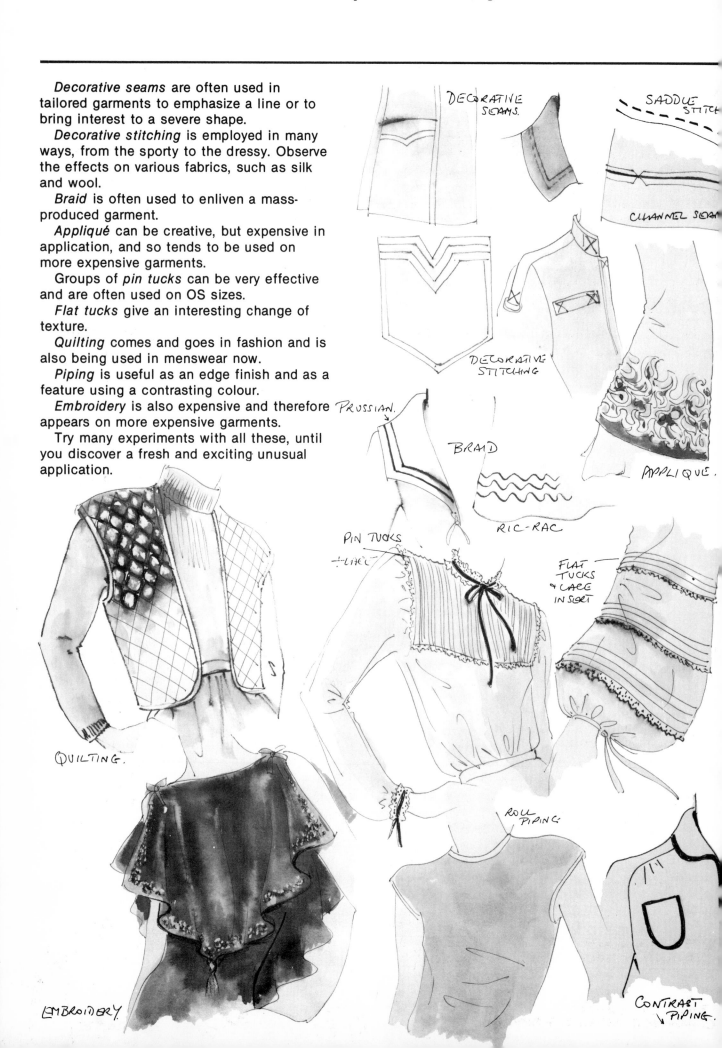

DECORATIVE SEAMS.

SADDLE STITCH

CHANNEL SEAM

DECORATIVE STITCHING

PRUSSIAN.

BRAID

RIC-RAC

APPLIQUE.

PIN TUCKS

FLAT TUCKS & LACE INSERT

QUILTING.

ROLL PIPING

EMBROIDERY.

CONTRAST PIPING

Detail

There are hundreds of pocket variations and here I illustrate a few basic styles. Study garments in shops and being worn, and analyse whether the pocket detail is right for the fabric.

In detail like tabs and epaulettes, it is advisable to accent one edge with shadow to indicate the detail is a separate piece. There are again many permutations of belt styles and I have only space to illustrate a few.

Details like bows can often provide a focal point to a design or accent a style feature. They occur time and time again in many forms and fabrics, and it is well to practise sketching bows in various fabrics.

From these basic themes many variations should be developed in your sketchbook.

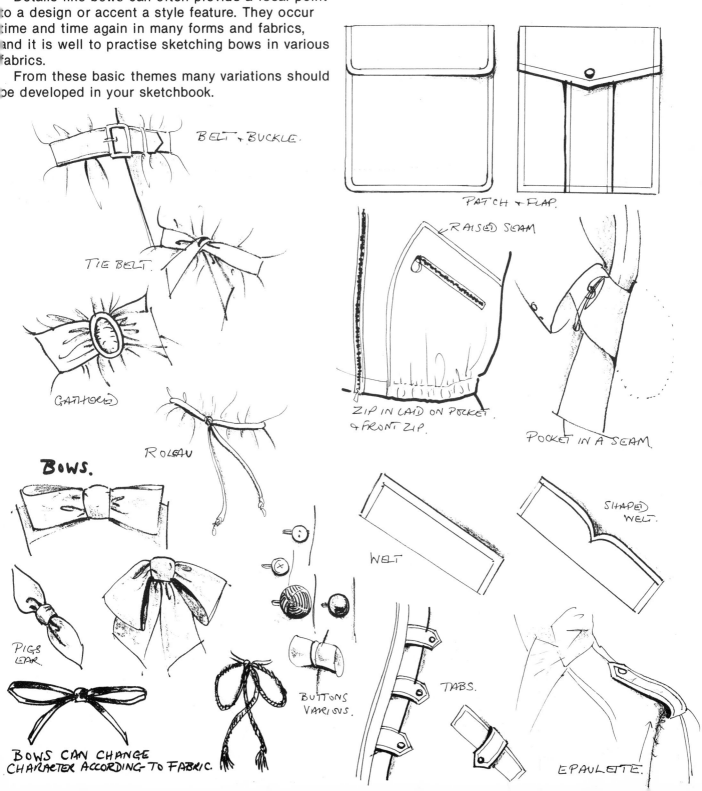

JETTED

CURVED JET.

PATCH + FLAP.

BELT + BUCKLE.

TIE BELT.

GATHERED

ROLEAU

RAISED SEAM

ZIP INLAID ON POCKET + FRONT ZIP.

POCKET IN A SEAM

WELT

SHAPED WELT.

BOWS.

PIGS EAR.

BUTTONS VARIOUS.

TABS.

EPAULETTE.

BOWS CAN CHANGE CHARACTER ACCORDING TO FABRIC.

Menswear: trousers

Note interesting presentation.
  Note interesting development of detail.
  When presenting finished ideas to a manufacturer or buyer it is essential they are visually attractive, easy to follow and show a professional approach.
  Courtesy of Nino publications.

Leger-Pants aus Sommer-Cottons

Die Hosenbeine stecken in Stiefeln oder derben Wollsocken!

Proportion and balance

o be an effective creative fashion designer it is
essential to master the basic fundamentals and
principles of design, before concentrating on
fashion looks. In this respect it is most important
o study the past masters of line, cut, shape and
silhouette.

Balenciaga
master of proportion and balance, allied to
structural shape and superb cut.

Chanel
Notable for the 'Chanel suit' shape, which goes on
and on. Masterly use of balance and proportion,
allied to clever detail and trim, with beautiful fabric
co-ordination, often tweeds with an exciting
character of their own.

Vionnet
The creator of the bias cut. These are clothes that
skim the body, flatter and enhance.

Molyneux
Master of understated elegance. Garments bought
in the 1930s are still being worn today.

Dior
Study the proportion and balance of the new look
of 1947.

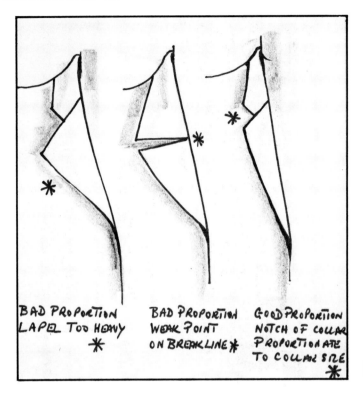

BAD PROPORTION LAPEL TOO HEAVY *

BAD PROPORTION WEAK POINT ON BREAKLINE *

GOOD PROPORTION NOTCH OF COLLAR PROPORTIONATE TO COLLAR SIZE *

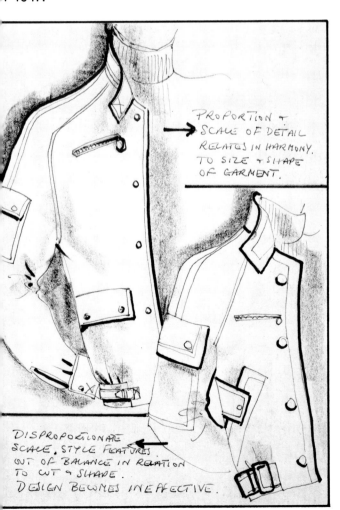

PROPORTION + SCALE OF DETAIL RELATES IN HARMONY TO SIZE + SHAPE OF GARMENT.

DISPROPORTIONATE SCALE, STYLE FEATURES. OUT OF BALANCE IN RELATION TO CUT + SHAPE. DESIGN BECOMES INEFFECTIVE.

Coming up to date, the aspiring designer should
study Cardin and St Laurent for consistent creative
ideas, not forgetting the Italian designers, for
example Lancetti with his superb use of prints, and
Valentino for his elegant tailored shapes.

If one examines Greek costume, the impression
is of tall elegant creatures although the Greeks
were probably no taller than we are today. The
vertical line of most of their costumes contributes
to this feeling of length and upward movement and
is echoed, of course, in the architecture of the
period. In fact, an interesting comparison can be
made of the relation of costume and architecture
in each period.

In many peasant costumes we have an emphasis
on the horizontal where the accent is on strength,
solidity and continuity. If one studies Tudor
costumes and those of, say, Philip IV of Spain and
the Spanish *infantas*, we note a heavy
curve ⌣⌣. This, incidentally, should be
used sparingly for it creates a heavy, portentous
look and in fact those people were often intent on
portraying superior status: the heavy solid
importance of wealth and position. The clothes
were made to emphasize this position of power.
Now as a contrast make a study of oriental
costume and note the effective use of a diagonal
line, often used to give a dramatic effect, allied to
rich contrasts in colour and texture.

As a designer one must be constantly searching
and analysing. One can be inspired by the unusual
or by the commonplace.

Line quality

The quality of line in a sketch is all important. A student can learn a great deal by comparing the work of two great fashion artists who have different approaches, for example, Paul Block (see *Women's Wear Daily*) and René Gruau (*Sir* and *International Textiles* leading advertisements).

The former has an economical fluidity of line and great style, conveying elegance and personality, whereas Gruau looks as if he was inspired by Toulouse-Lautrec and has great dash, *brio* and impact.

There are underlying rules to consider when using line and combinations of lines in a design:

Vertical lines suggest height and length.

Horizontal lines suggest width and stability and can make the figure look wider.

Diagonal lines can be used in a dramatic way to suggest movement or in OS to minimize and break up bulk in volume.

Heavy curves can look clumsy and bulky and must be used with discretion.

Longer curves suggest a more pleasant flowing movement, rhythm and harmony.

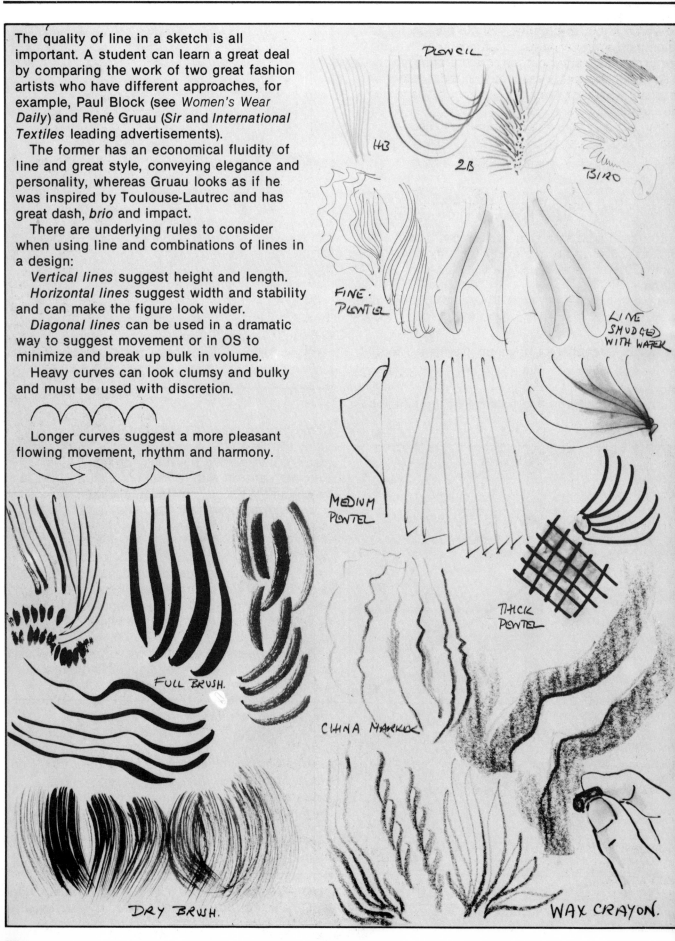

PENCIL

H3

2B

BIRO

FINE PENTEL

LINE SMUDGED WITH WATER

MEDIUM PENTEL

THICK PENTEL

FULL BRUSH.

CHINA MARKER

DRY BRUSH.

WAX CRAYON.

Pattern and texture

xperiment with wax crayon, conté crayon, hina marker, charcoal and Caron d'Ache encil to achieve various effects.

For print designs I used Pentel and wash. o not overwork a print or you will flatten he subject and lose spontaneity.

Sheer fabrics are often shown over a more paque foundation and a two-tone wash ombined with fine pen was used in this nstance.

For the effect of lace I used pen and wax rayon. Again lace is often shown over a slip f silk, taffeta or poult.

Stripes can be shown in various ways, one f the easiest being to use wax and then pply a half-tone wash with a full brush.

PRINT

SHEERS

LACE

STRIPES

SINGLE JERSEY

Jersey fabric (in this case fine polyester single jersey) must look fluid and flowing. Here I used wax crayon; other artists might prefer conté, charcoal or china marker pencil.

More basic poses

Sketch many examples of basic poses and experiment with hair styles, shoes, etc., to achieve a current fashion look.

Here I used a medium Pentel and wash.

Here I used a fine Pentel and employed white wax on a grained paper for highlighting hair and legs and also to give the effect of lurex tights. I then used a medium wash of Quink ink and, finally, a darker tone for the body garment.

Menswear
Practise presenting a group or variations on a theme. Select from your rough notes several poses and experiment on a separate sheet interlocking and overlapping the figures to achieve an interesting pattern and balance, while not obscuring any important design feature.

Freelance design to a brief (continued)

This group of three shirt designs was executed in pen and wash in a style that would be suitable for presentation to a buyer. Diagrammatic back views are presented as a unit.

Taking the menswear shirt design opposite, I have presented the same design in a much more free and distinctive style suitable for magazine illustration. Comparing the two sketches you will notice that this example is more eye-catching and has more style. The sketch was executed with brush and ink and half-tone wash.

Points to consider
Look for a pose that will accentuate the main style features and emphasize them. Consider the inclusion of relevant fashion accessories (in this case a narrow knitted tie).

Ladies' skirt design development

This shows an excellent example of presenting development ideas on ladies' skirt themes. Note the young look fashion figures and the clear and attractive diagrammatic presentation of the variations. Also the inclusion of swatch and fabric specifications. The whole thing looks crisp and professional with a strong designer feeling.

Note in the various skirts how weight and volume is well portrayed. Pleats, gathers and folds are all clearly shown and defined.

Courtesy of Nino publications.

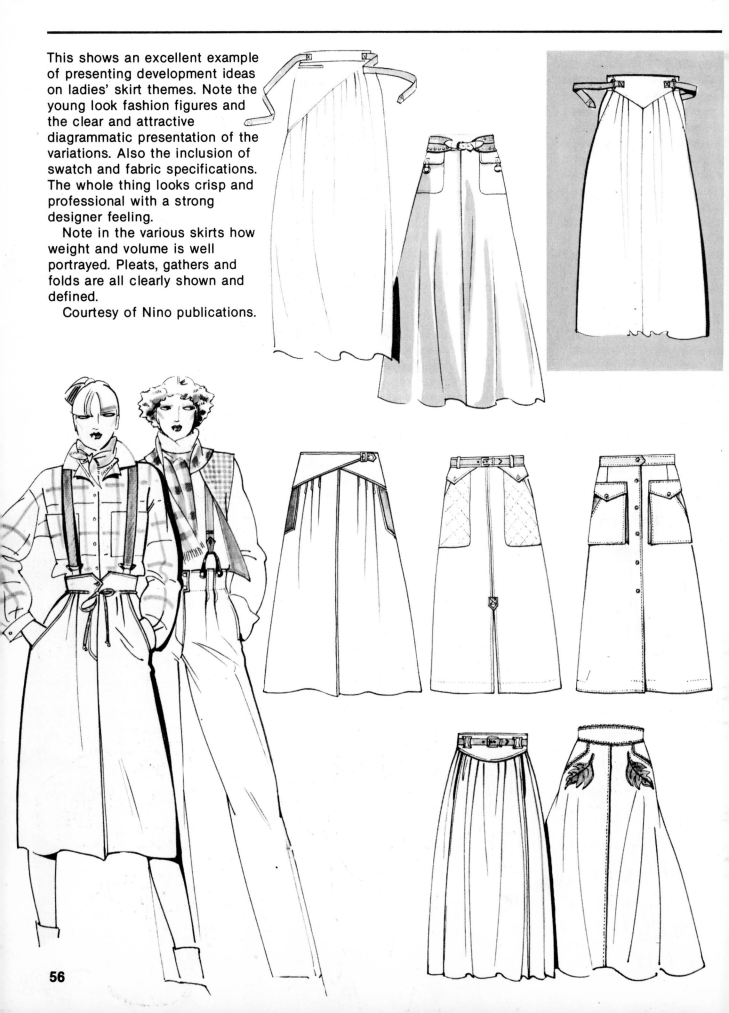

Ladies' blouse design development

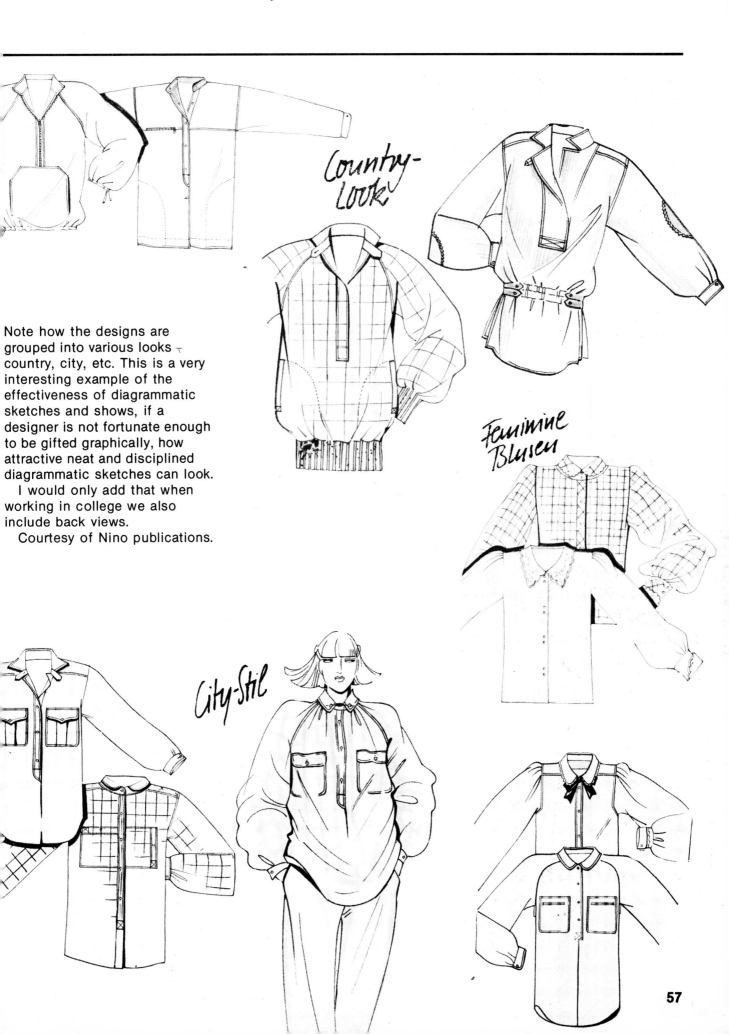

Country-Look

Feminine Blusen

City-Stil

Note how the designs are grouped into various looks – country, city, etc. This is a very interesting example of the effectiveness of diagrammatic sketches and shows, if a designer is not fortunate enough to be gifted graphically, how attractive neat and disciplined diagrammatic sketches can look.

I would only add that when working in college we also include back views.

Courtesy of Nino publications.

Ladies' trouser design development

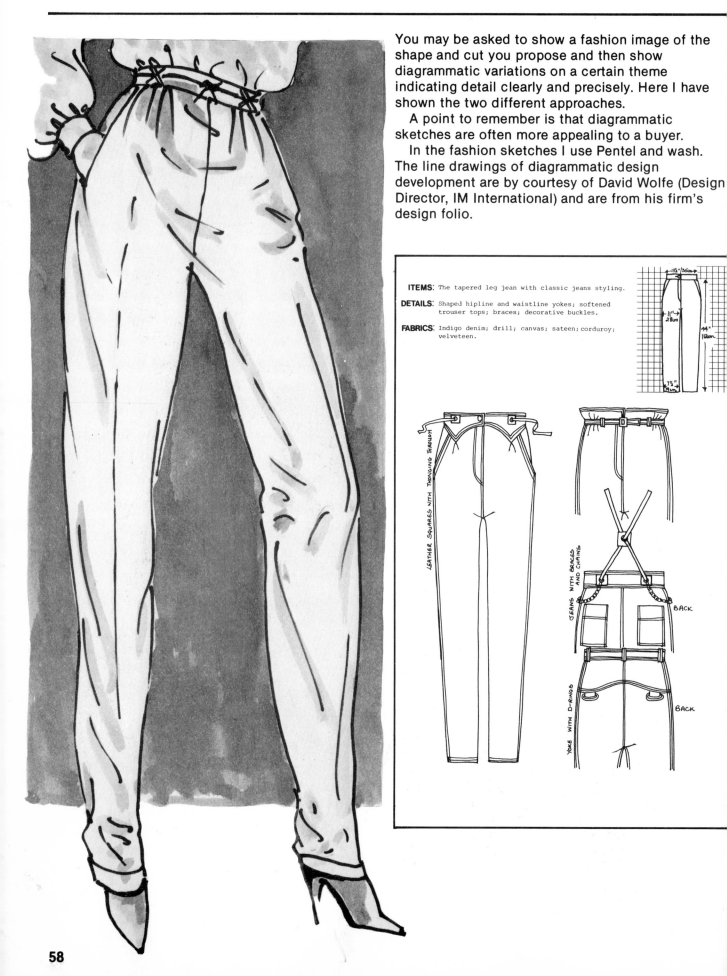

You may be asked to show a fashion image of the shape and cut you propose and then show diagrammatic variations on a certain theme indicating detail clearly and precisely. Here I have shown the two different approaches.

A point to remember is that diagrammatic sketches are often more appealing to a buyer.

In the fashion sketches I use Pentel and wash. The line drawings of diagrammatic design development are by courtesy of David Wolfe (Design Director, IM International) and are from his firm's design folio.

ITEMS: The tapered leg jean with classic jeans styling.

DETAILS: Shaped hipline and waistline yokes; softened trouser tops; braces; decorative buckles.

FABRICS: Indigo denim; drill; canvas; sateen; corduroy; velveteen.

LEATHER SQUARES WITH THONGING THROUGH

JEANS WITH BRACES AND CHAINS

YOKE WITH D-RINGS

BACK

BACK

Design development

Variations on a theme: rough
design development of casual
coordinates.

SWATCHES

SAMPLE.

Menswear: unstructured

This is a very instructive sheet for an aspiring menswear designer.

Note how the weight and bulk of the silhouette changes and, in the second sketch of the collarless jacket, how subtly the new shape is indicated. Here again, for studio work I would personally add diagrammatic back views.

Courtesy of Nino publications.

Menswear: shirt design

This is an excellent theme to work on, showing first a fashion image and then a breakdown of detail presented in blocks and showing the salient design details.

Note how the poses vary and are complementary. The clarity and character of these sheets are an indication of what a fashion design student should strive for. The rough sheets can be more experimental and free in style.

Courtesy of Nino publications.

Fashion design: conclusion

Job analysis

Be prepared to be 'adaptable' to the style of your company.

Keep abreast of current trends in fashion and fabric.

Work closely with the sample machinist.

Be aware of production problems.

Acquire some knowledge of grading.

Be conversant with all aspects of costing.

Be aware of colour trends and take this into consideration when selecting alternative colourways for a style included in the range.

Be aware of new fabric developments.

Design studio

You may work alone or as part of a team and will usually be responsible to design/sales directors. Some firms produce many samples and then decide on a limited range. Other firms have frequent range meetings and quickly eliminate non-starters. Still other firms work closely with store buyers to produce or adapt the look they want.

You must learn to cope with intransigent buyers.

It will be necessary to produce competent patterns with all balance notches and relevant information for if these are not correct at the first stage, a later bulk quantity may be cut and found to be wrong.

Usually one has the opportunity to go abroad two or three times a year to shows. Take the opportunity to do some market research on these trips, as it can be a great stimulus and also of great practical value.

Fashion illustration

Many students confuse fashion design and fashion illustration.

Fashion design

The aim here is to show an attractive graphic presentation of a design revealing the shape, proportion and detail; all cutting and seam lines should be in proportion. Always give front and back views and an indication of the fabric and colour to be used in the design. A cutter should be able to interpret the idea into a pattern without recourse to the artist.

Fashion illustration

This must have impact and catch the eye of anyone flicking through the pages of a magazine or paper. The sketch must project an idea or theme and sell the idea. Some aspects involve exaggeration but there is great expertise in knowing what to emphasize. Some fashion drawings look disarmingly casual as if they have been sketched in a few minutes. Many students are puzzled by this and surprised when told their fashion sketches look tight and overworked. Today the style of both fashion and fashion drawings changes quickly and a fashion artist must be aware of all new trends and developments.

Let your own personal style develop naturally, but build on what has been done before. Experiment continually.

Fashion illustration (continued)

The fashion illustrator must be able to draw the human figure with complete assurance. Fashion illustration is a very competitive and overcrowded field and any student who wishes to succeed as a fashion artist must be able to assess his own work and take expert advice as to whether he has the necessary graphic skills allied to a strong fashion sense. Many people with no formal training are also competing with trained students in this area. I am often asked by students who have shown their work to an art studio or agent, 'Why did they say my work was too tight?' They find it difficult to appreciate that the current fashion drawing look is mainly for a casual throw away look, spontaneous and with lots of *brio* and panache. It has to look as if the sketch was dashed off in ten minutes, whereas in actual fact there is much preparation and often the sketch has been done several times to achieve the sparkle and freshness. In this respect a student's work often looks wooden and lifeless. I have seen the work of many well known fashion artists. Often bits of paper are pieced together, or mistakes are blocked out as one part of the sketch does not work out but the rest is successful. The look of the original sketch does not matter, it is how it looks when printed that is important.

When illustrating, one must adopt a different technique of presentation for different areas of the market or advertisement. It is advisable to build a file of a wide variety of advertisements from magazines and newspapers, colour and black and white. It is rare for a beginner to have the opportunity of working in colour as the reproduction costs are very high. Most work is done in line, in black and white and half-tone, or half-tone and one colour.

The essential differences between a design drawing and a fashion sketch are shown in this book. The design drawing is done primarily to show the shape, cut, detail, trim and proportion, clearly and legibly for the cutter or buyer. A fashion drawing must have impact, project the main line of the silhouette (and fashion look) and be sufficiently eye-catching for someone to think 'I would like to buy that'. So it is advisable to study the work of as many fashion artists as possible, to compare different styles and analyse whether they succeed or not. The old cliché that 'practice makes perfect' still applies and a hopeful fashion artist must experiment with all the techniques suggested and eventually develop a personal style. It may appear rather contradictory that being too way out may prevent a beginner getting fashion work but that eventually the originality of style lifts the artist up the scale. One of the best examples is René Gruau. This artist knows the value of every nuance and, most important, what to leave out. Most students overwork their early attempts and their work consequently looks laboured and contrived.

Apart from fashion work for advertisements there are now quite a number of studios which offer a fashion service in portfolio form. Quite a lot of this work is done by freelance artists, who are given the fashion designs and have to present several designs on a large sheet in an attractive manner. They usually prepare a rough and if this is accepted, they complete the finished work.

The American fashion paper, *Women's Wear Daily*, is renowned for using brilliant fashion artists and should be closely studied. The equivalent British paper, *Fashion Weekly*, often uses first class fashion artists like David Wolfe and Colin Barnes.

There are of course fashion studios which specialize in certain areas and the experience of working for them can be invaluable to the young artist. The names and addresses can be obtained from *Artists' and Writers' Year Book*.

I outline in this section of the book some techniques which one should experiment with and develop, gradually building up an interesting and varied cross-section of work.

Basic poses: women

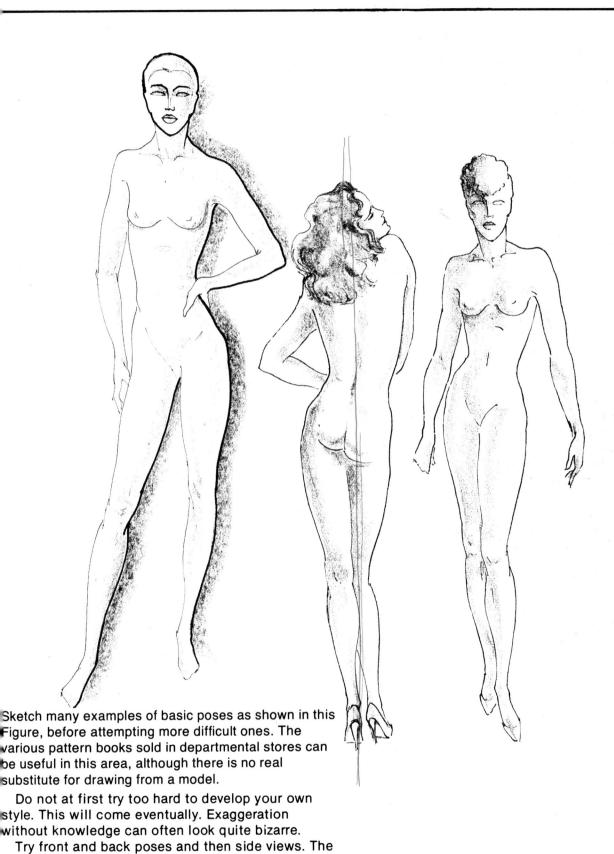

Sketch many examples of basic poses as shown in this
Figure, before attempting more difficult ones. The
various pattern books sold in departmental stores can
be useful in this area, although there is no real
substitute for drawing from a model.

Do not at first try too hard to develop your own
style. This will come eventually. Exaggeration
without knowledge can often look quite bizarre.

Try front and back poses and then side views. The
most important aspect in drawing the human figure
is to avoid a wooden or frozen look. The figure must
have rhythm and keep in mind the form of the letter
S.

If a model is not available, you will probably have
to resort to the use of photographs but there are
many pitfalls here, such as the distortion of form by
lighting.

Basic poses: men

Sketch many similar basic poses initially! Do not try to be too adventurous until you have mastered some basic themes.

Draw from models or photographs and experiment with various techniques: soft pencil, Pentel and wash and wax crayon.

Avoid a static wooden look and aim at a feeling of rhythm in the figure. The two poses shown here are good for casual wear and were sketched firstly in pencil and then pen and wash.

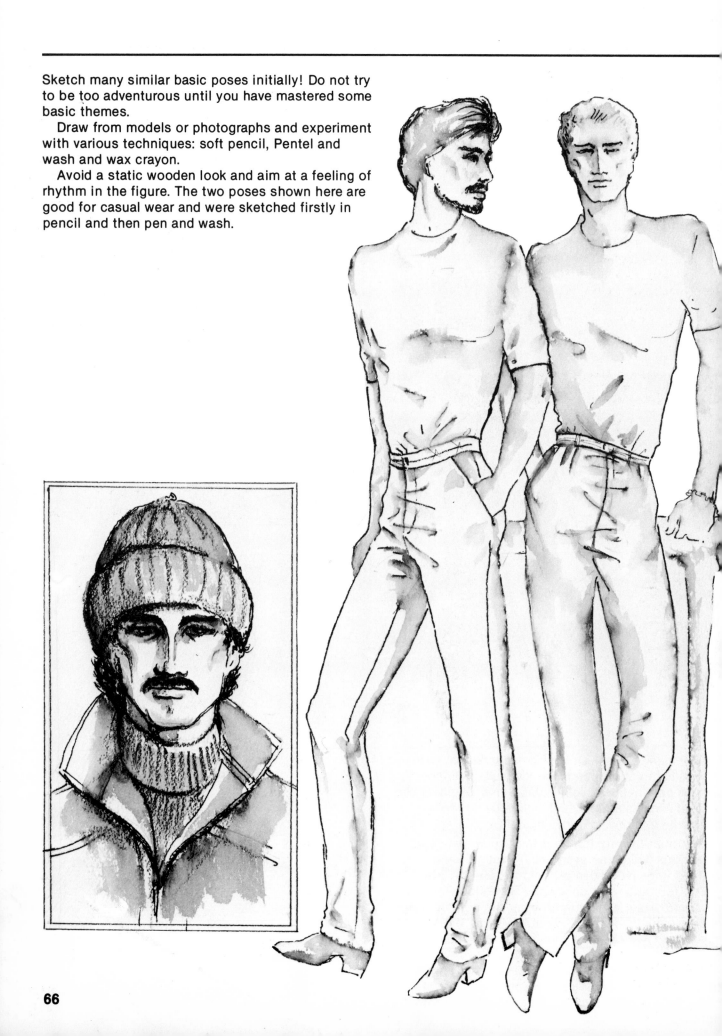

The face: basic proportion as a guide

Sketch an egg shape and divide approximately in half for position of the eyes.

Divide as shown in sketch B.

If faces are not your strong point, then practise this many times, until the details fit into place almost automatically.

Draw from various models, before experimenting with techniques.

C is sketched with black wax crayon and is meant to represent a young sporty image. D and E project something of a glamour look and were produced by pen and wash.

You must vary the image of the face according to the pose and type of garment to be illustrated. In the sketch at lower left we see the variation to be indicated when sketching a female and a male face.

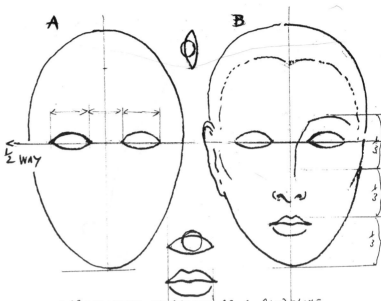

A

B

½ WAY

APPROXIMATE MEASURES AS A GUIDELINE.

C

WAX CRAYON.

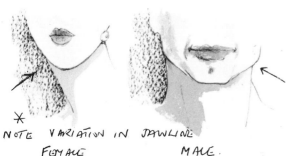

* NOTE VARIATION IN JAWLINE
FEMALE   MALE.

LOOKING UP FROM
BELOW EYE LEVEL

D

E

LOOKING DOWN FROM.
ABOVE EYE
LEVEL.

PEN & WASH

The face: detail

It is advisable to practise individual details before attempting a full face.

Start with the lips. It is better in the initial stages to draw faces with natural shape and proportion. Stylization can develop at a later stage. Accentuate the division of the lips and do not sketch a thin lower lip.

For the eye, draw an almond shape and then lightly define the pupil as shown. Build up from there by thickening the line for the upper lid and eyelashes. By applying a soft shadow at the corner and outer tip of the eye, you can create the illusion of depth.

Generally speaking the ear and the nose are toned down in fashion sketches, as they can easily become too insistent.

Check the subtle line of the neck into the shoulder. This is the line that often appears difficult to many people.

Now try drawing a three-quarter face and finally a profile.

* IMPORTANT
PRACTICE LINE OF NECK - 'CHIN TO SHOULDER'

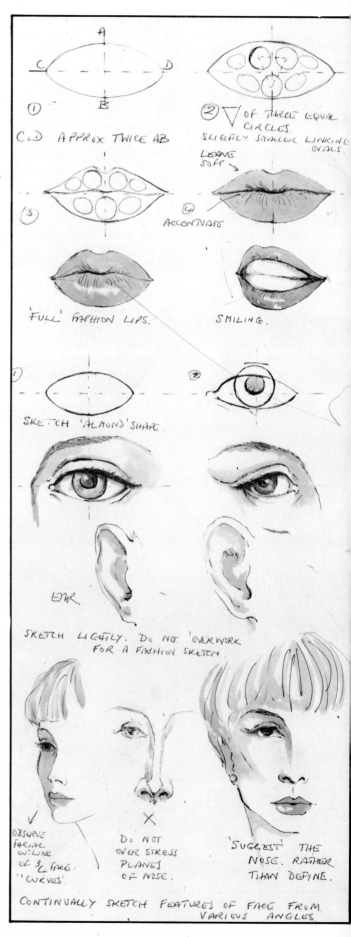

① $C \cdot D$ APPROX TWICE AB

② OF THREE EQUAL CIRCLES. SLIGHTLY SMALLER LINKING OVALS. LEAVE SOFT →

③

④ ACCENTUATE

'FULL' FASHION LIPS.

SMILING.

① SKETCH 'ALMOND' SHAPE

②

EAR.

SKETCH LIGHTLY. DO NOT 'OVERWORK' FOR A FASHION SKETCH.

✓ OBSERVE FACIAL OUTLINE OF ¾ FACE. 'CURVES'

✗ DO NOT OVER STRESS PLANES OF NOSE.

'SUGGEST' THE NOSE. RATHER THAN DEFINE.

CONTINUALLY SKETCH FEATURES OF FACE FROM VARIOUS ANGLES

The fashion face

The examples shown are all sketched with wax crayon, apart from the example marked with an asterisk.

Sketch many examples in wax or conté then try to eliminate superfluous detail. I appreciate that wax crayon or conté may not suit everyone, so if you find this difficult use a soft pencil or china marker. The disadvantage with a hard pencil, for example, 2H, is that one tends to get a thin spidery look, whereas a sketch with wax or conté gives a more natural effect. If one glances at a face the effect is of soft shadows defining the detail rather than a hard edge.

Men's faces

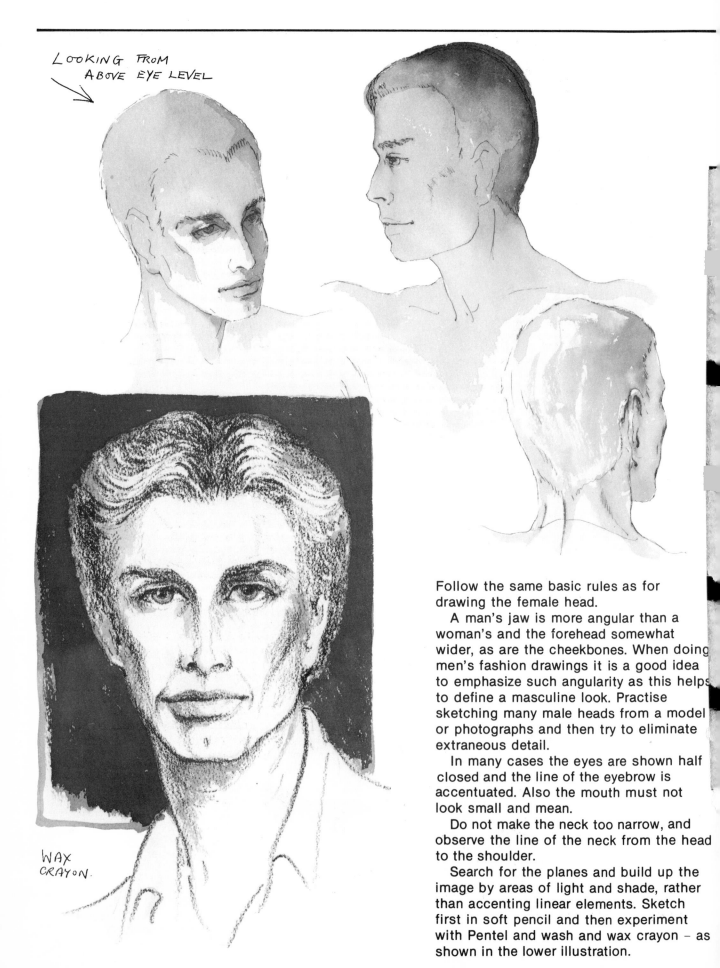

LOOKING FROM ABOVE EYE LEVEL

WAX CRAYON.

Follow the same basic rules as for drawing the female head.

A man's jaw is more angular than a woman's and the forehead somewhat wider, as are the cheekbones. When doing men's fashion drawings it is a good idea to emphasize such angularity as this helps to define a masculine look. Practise sketching many male heads from a model or photographs and then try to eliminate extraneous detail.

In many cases the eyes are shown half closed and the line of the eyebrow is accentuated. Also the mouth must not look small and mean.

Do not make the neck too narrow, and observe the line of the neck from the head to the shoulder.

Search for the planes and build up the image by areas of light and shade, rather than accenting linear elements. Sketch first in soft pencil and then experiment with Pentel and wash and wax crayon – as shown in the lower illustration.

Men's features: stylization

SKETCH FROM MODEL

STAGE _II_ STYLIZATION

STAGE _III_ STYLIZATION

Sequence:
1. Sketch from model
2. Overlay tracing paper and redraw, eliminating shading
3. Overlay tracing paper and try and sketch only essential lines

Rhythm and movement

Certain garments, particularly sporty ones, can be more effectively sketched if there is some movement in the figure. Students should practise some basic poses with movement and then experiment with various types of garments and fabrics on these figures. These should give an immediate impression of the character and type of fabric, from heavy tweed to clinging jersey.

Note how the fabric swirls round the lower female figure, as the figure appears to move forward.

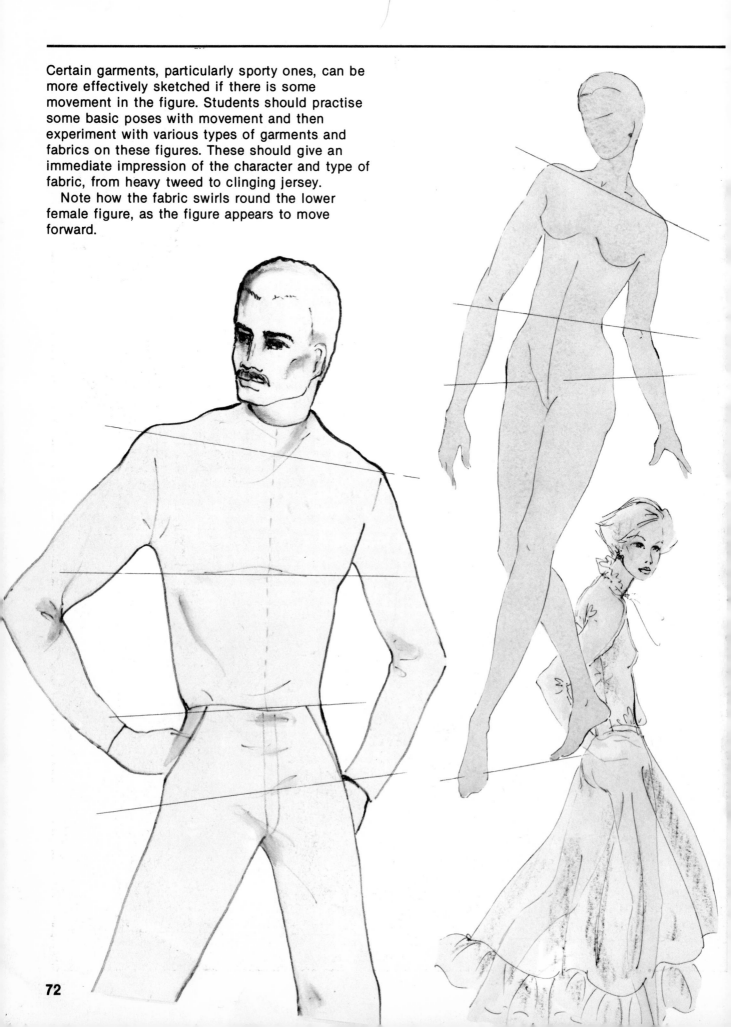

Hands and feet

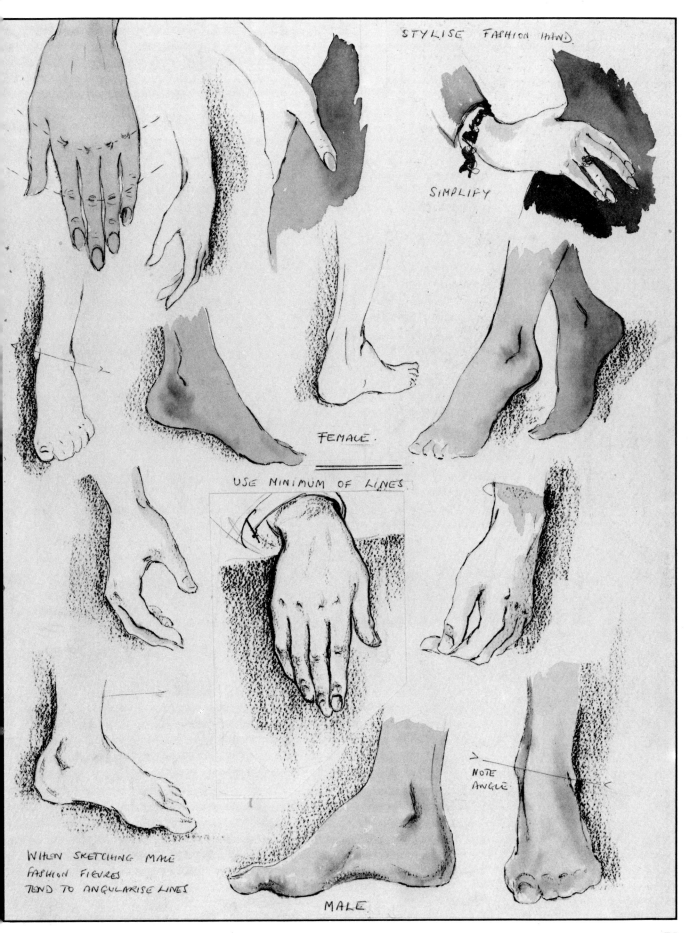

STYLISE FASHION HAND

SIMPLIFY

FEMALE.

USE MINIMUM OF LINES

NOTE ANGLE

WHEN SKETCHING MALE
FASHION FIGURES
TEND TO ANGULARISE LINES

MALE

Shoes and boots

WHITE & BLACK WAX + FINE + MEDIUM FELT PEN. GREY WASH

Accessories

Plan the page in an interesting and well balanced format, making sure all details of design and shape are evident and yet a visually eye-catching scheme is designed.
  Note that a certain amount of black helps to accentuate the shape of the bags.

Technique
After roughing out in pencil I used a medium and fine Pentel and mid-tone grey wash, using white wax again for highlights.

Lingerie

This technique can be used effectively for dramatic emphasis or to illustrate pale or translucent fabric.

Technique
First of all I produced a light pencil sketch using a photograph as the starting point because a model was not available. Using this as a base, I then went over the sketch with a fine water soluble Pentel and erased the pencil line.

Sketch 1   I then mixed a half-tone wash (half ink, half water) and applied this in a generous wash with a full brush, leaving the area of the hair with a fluffy irregular edge.

Sketch 2   Then I applied a deeper tone of wash in the background to outline the figure.

Sketch 3   Using white gouache I then built up the shape of the garment, using the half-tone again for folds and shadows. Finally for lace detail I went over the lace with a fine black Pentel.

Design by Maggie Clarke adapted from a photograph by courtesy of *Fashion Weekly*.

Design trends: avant-garde

These examples are from the
International Institute for Cotton
fashion folio menswear which, as in
other studios, is produced to show
an indication of future trends.
 By courtesy of the International
Institute for Cotton.

Adaptation of style to market requirements

Mail-order approach
Show clearly, at a glance, all details of style, proportion and shape.
Give a clear indication of pattern or texture.
Convey the right mood.
'Sell' the design to the prospective buyer.

Fashion magazine approach
Catch the eye of anyone skimming through the magazine.
Dramatize the important features.
Convey an impression of pattern or texture.
Convey the impression that the garment would be attractive on the reader.
Fashion feeling is more important than detail.

Developing a style

These superb sketches by David Wolfe are an indication of style trends and were produced for the excellent IM International Fashion Folio. They also show the student how the clever use of the right pose can enhance the design, and the detail and texture are clearly indicated. The sketches are not over-exaggerated and are very attractive, arresting and easy to 'read'.

By courtesy of David Wolfe, Creative Director of IM International.

FRINGE EMBROIDERY STUDS

CLASSIC BLOUSON

LAMB

GILET

FELT

LEATHER

FAKE FUR

TRIMS

BRIGHT RED

CREPE DE CHINE

RUFFLED

POWDER BLUE

SAP GREEN

ASYMMETRIC

DRAPE

STOCK TIE

JUTE - SOFT JADE - DARK GREEN

ONE BUTTON

OXFORD CLOTH

WOOL CREPE

WOOL VOILE

RASPBERRY ICE

CREPE GEORGETTE

ROMANTIC

SHIRT

UPDATED SHIRT

COORDINATED SHIRT AND KIMONO

LAVENDER WATER NAVY-GREY-LEMON TWIST

HIPSTER MINI

TOPSTITCH STRETCH GABERDINE

WOOL CHALLIS

GREY

TIERS, DIAGONAL

ORANGE PEKOE-NAVY-GREY PRINT

YOKE

BLACK-GREY FLANNEL

BELL SHAPE

SLATE-NAVY-CHINA BLUE

BLANKET WOOL

BORDER WRAP

SELF FRINGE

RUSSET-BLACK BORDER

PLEATS

SPIRAL WRAP

WOOL CREPE

JEANS JACKET

PRINT LINING

LO-RISE

JEANS

BLACK DENIM

HARLEQUIN: STEM GINGER, ORANGE PEKOE, ORANGE BLOSSOM

PRINT

VELOUR

LO-RISE BAGGY

SMOKE SUEDE

WIDE

HIPSTER

JUTE DOUBLEKNIT

BAGGY

PLUS FOURS

DONKEY VELVETEEN

Groups: menswear

There are occasions when one has to illustrate three or four garments in a limited space and sometimes the assignment will include suggesting a setting or background.

Experiment with placing figures in a harmonious group. Obviously if there is no relevant design detail on the lower part of the figure, it is unnecessary to show this in the sketch. Where the work includes several figures in a setting, it is usual to submit a rough first for approval, before attempting any finished work.

Fur

Technique

Sketch very lightly the style and pose in pencil, then apply a wash of clear water to the shape. As this dries off, apply a medium wash following the shadows of fur.

When almost dry, add deeper tones with ink and water.

When quite dry, pick out edges with a soft pencil. Complete the details of face and head scarf.

Fabric technique: man's suit

Sketch the figure lightly in pencil. Using Quink ink and a number 7 sable brush, sketch in the shape and detail.

With white wax indicate diagonal twill or repp line. Accent the left side where light strikes and less in the shadows.

Brush all over with a full brush, a half-tone grey and allow to dry.

Paint in the frame outline in deeper tone.

Co-ordinates

Up-market co-ordinated, tweed
   and jersery ensemble.
Single jersey top, with cowl
   collar and fringe edge.
Double jersey overpull.
Striped dirndl-type skirt and
   tweed topcoat.
   Aim   To project in the sketch
an elegant casual outdoor look –
hence the windswept hair. Also
to dramatize a garment that
could easily look boring. I used a
fairly rough semi-absorbent paper
and after several roughs decided
on the pose and roughed this in,
in soft pencil. I then used a
number 7 sable brush to outline
the pose and style and white
wax to indicate the flecks of the
tweed and the stripes in the
skirt. Using a full brush and half-
tone wash I then briskly washed
in the main areas of light and
shade, and used a wax crayon to
give the effect of windswept hair.
Finally a dark accent at the lower
end of the sketch indicated an
outdoor feeling.

Fashion Folio International trend sketches

As I discussed earlier, many firms take one or more of the fashion folios produced by various studios as a guide to new trends and fabric developments.

Shown here and opposite are two pages from Benjamin Dent's Fashion Folio Folder for autumn/winter 1984/5.

Illustration by courtesy of Benjamin Dent Ltd, Fashion Folio International, 33 Bedford Place, WC1B 5JX.

Women's sportswear

These illustrations of ladies' sportswear by Nino have strong impact and show an interesting use of contrast.

Note how the pose for the golf style immediately tells the observer of the sport indicated.

Note also how a judicious use of shadow here and there, can give the figure substance.

Courtesy of Nino publications.

Sketching from life

Swimwear
The first two sketches are from a model wearing a
swimsuit. It is very important to sketch from a
model whenever possible.

Design development

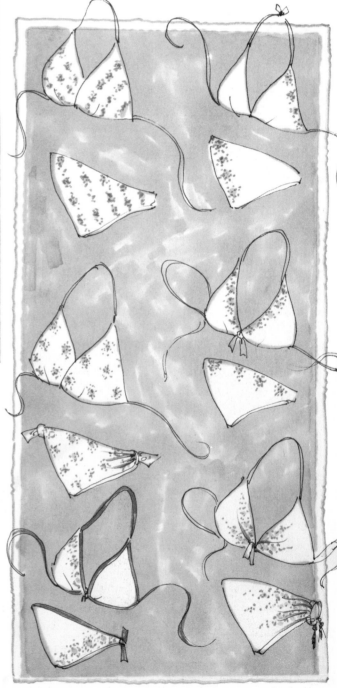

When showing variations of the original idea it is not necessary to sketch all the figure or head, particularly if you are not strong on sketching faces.

Diagrammatic sketches again illustrate the variations on a theme and I have blocked out the variations with a light-blue felt marker. The felt markers are expensive, but do give a slick professional finish.

The large final sketch on tinted paper is intended to show the idea for a fashion paper or magazine. The garment should be the first thing to strike the attention and the figure is subsidiary. The pose should be selected to enhance the design. First I sketched in pencil, then used a fine brush and ink to outline the figure and used white body colour on the swimsuit.

Summer dresses

Here we assume that we are illustrating an article on summer dresses. Often these might be quite simple and need dramatizing.

The main effect was to achieve spontaneity and freshness. The sketch should not look tight or overworked. The word to keep in mind is 'impact'. Again we strive for rhythm and movement to give a swish to the line of the skirt.

The two sketches shown were sketched directly with felt pen without any preliminary pencil rough.

Drapery

In this case I used a tinted paper, Quink ink, wax and white acrylic. When doing a drawing of this kind, one tries to achieve a natural flowing line and to select a pose that will enhance the features of the design.

Experiment with various techniques and study the designs of Vionnet, Alix-Grès, Molyneux, Yuki.

Disco wear

One fashion that is now developing with the feeling for body clothes is the return to stretch fabrics that cling to the figure. The structure of the fabric is usually stretch-knitted and is often worn with some type of loose overgarment that can be discarded for disco-dancing.

For this illustration one must use a pose that emphasizes movement and rhythm and here we find how important the study of life drawing is to a fashion artist. Sketch several guide poses from the model. Separate sketches may be necessary for positions of feet, arms and hands. I used a semi-absorbent tinted paper and first of all sketched the pose in pen and ink. A white wax was then used to show highlights and texture of lurex and to indicate the movement of the fringe overskirt. I then applied a half-tone wash over the body garment and when this was dry, a deeper-to-black tone over the background.

Evening wear

The man's suit is a dull, heavy-weight satin by Basile, and the lady's evening dress from Jean Louis Scherrer combines the structural and decorative, and has strong echoes from the 1950s.

I used a heavy-weight medium-smooth paper and faintly mapped out the figure positions before applying a generous wash of mid-tone Quink ink and water.

I then worked in the main areas of mid-tone and built up the white dress with body colour and finally applied the fine detail with a pen.

Fashion illustration: conclusion

Building a portfolio

Produce a good cross-section of work: women's, children's, men's.

Cover all aspects, day wear, sports, casuals, knitwear, formal, town, country, etc.

Show a wide variety of techniques.

Show various styles for various markets, for example, magazine and mail-order.

Have several black and white, line only drawings.

Have several half-tone drawings.

Show versatility and adaptability.

Try to achieve a lively spontaneous look and do not overwork drawings.

A small percentage of drawings should be in full colour.

Try to show treatment of various fabrics.

Be sure to project a current fashion look.

Check accessory details.

Do not show examples that are too small.

Make sure the sketches have impact.

For specimens, work mainly on thick paper or fashion boards.

Study the work of famous fashion artists, for example:

Erté, Lepape, René Gruau, Francis Marshall, Barbara Hulanicki, Rix, Tod Draz, Paul Christodoulou, Jacques Demachy, Stemp, May Routh, Peake, Bouche, Eric, Pedro Barrios, Kenneth Paul Block, Robert Passantino, Steven Stipelman, Elizabeth Suter, David Wolfe, Colin Barnes, Dorothy Loverro, Robert Young.